The Risk Business

What CISOs Need to Know About Risk-Based Cybersecurity

By Levi Gundert
Foreword by Stu Solomon

With editorial assistance from
Zane Pokorny and Jeff May

CYBEREDGE
P R E S S

The Risk Business: What CISOs Need to Know About Risk-Based Cybersecurity
CyberEdge Group, LLC
1997 Annapolis Exchange Parkway
Suite 300
Annapolis, MD 21401
(800) 327-8711
www.cyber-edge.com

For general information on CyberEdge Group research and marketing consulting services, or to create a custom *Definitive Guide* book for your organization, contact our sales department at 800-327-8711 or info@cyber-edge.com.

ISBN: 978-1-948939-13-3 (paperback)
ISBN: 978-1-948939-14-0 (eBook)

Printed in the United States of America.

10 9 8 7 6 5 4 3 2 1

Publisher's Acknowledgements

CyberEdge Group thanks the following individuals for their respective contributions:

Copy Editor: Susan Shuttleworth
Graphic Designer: Debbi Stocco
Production Coordinator: Jon Friedman

Foreword

I t is my pleasure and honor to recommend this work as essential reading for both technically astute and business-minded security practitioners, and for all of us who work as a community to protect the availability and integrity of our systems, data, and operations from malicious cyber actors.

For nearly 20 years, I have watched our security industry struggle to strike the right balance between the technical tools of our trade — usually complex, sometimes elegant, and often expensive — and the practical outcomes we try to achieve. As is so often the case in our industry, the predominant topic of discussion is technical controls and tools. This focus, while necessary (and let's face it, the source of great job and wealth creation for ourselves and so many of our colleagues and friends), actually distracts from the core solution that we must embrace: a holistic approach to security intelligence.

This approach requires an evolution toward risk-based cyber-security. It is predicated on the ability to express the value of security activities in terms of measurable and defined out-comes based on risk reduction. It also requires a rich under-standing of the threat environment, a clear appreciation of the concept of criticality, and an awareness of the potential impact of cyberattacks from an operational business standpoint.

In this book, my close friend and colleague Levi Gundert deftly bridges the chasm between technology and focused risk reduction. He describes how to create an environment where operational risk is identified and managed down to an accept-able level. Levi reviews core concepts of traditional intelligence and describes advanced techniques that can be used to identify and quantify threats based on adversary activity, intent, and capabilities. The end result is a clearer picture of the risks posed to enterprises by malicious cyber actors.

To address the normally slippery topic of risk calculation, Levi takes the reader through a tight and practical exercise on how to effectively identify, calculate, and apply risk-based concepts when executing an intelligence-led and risk-informed security strategy. He interweaves real-world examples collected during a decades-long career in federal law enforcement, the financial sector, and the security start-up community. His unique experiences are conveyed effortlessly and with great conviction in this work.

I encourage you to use this book as a practical guide and apply its ideas to your strategic and operational security challenges. Its lessons are actionable: use them to break down problems into bite-sized chunks, enrich your understanding of the threat environment, make decisions with business criticality and operational context in mind, and take actions that are measured and focused on risk reduction.

Stu Solomon
Chief, Intelligence Solutions — Recorded Future
Charlotte, NC
February 2020

Table of Contents

Acknowledgements

This book was largely written with T-Rex arm posture on a tray table somewhere north of 30,000 feet while crossing the United States or a large stretch of ocean. However, I also spent time holed up in my office writing on nights and weekends, and I'm grateful to my beautiful wife, Sarah, my three charming children, and my kind in-laws for their love and their patience with me.

I also want to thank the mentors in my life who were instrumental in imparting wisdom and supporting me during various periods of my career, including Steve Lamb, Andy Bechtle, Rabbi Rob Thomas, Gavin Reid, Stu Solomon, and Dr. Christopher Ahlberg.

I've worked for incredible organizations stocked with smart and talented people throughout my professional journey. Recorded Future stands out for its exceptional, continual pursuit of solutions to customer problems. I'm enormously blessed to work daily with Futurists (my colleagues at Recorded Future) while attempting to contribute to a software product that is always improving. Thank you, Recorded Future, for all the memories and for assistance with this effort.

I'm especially grateful to Zane Pokorny for his energy and editorial attention while turning this effort into a real book.

Finally, this book would not be possible without the considerable influence and review of the following titans who helped shape my thinking, sometimes over a beverage at a conference networking event or after work: Dr. Bill Ladd, Rene White, Dr. Staffan Truve, Matt Kodama, Marie Brattberg, Petter Eriksson, Chris Holden, Maggie McDaniel, Dan Bearl, John Wetzel, Denver Durham, Dan Kropp, Gili Gonczarowski, Ryan Baker,

Mike Carney, Jason Giorgi, Thien Huynh, Andrew Scott, Faith Oliver, John "Four" Flynn, Stephan Chenette, Julie Starnes, Tyler Bradshaw, Rachel Adam, Jerry Dixon, Bill Powell, Andrew Tsonchev, Dan Wissman, Craig Williams, Daniel Hatheway, and all of Recorded Future's Intelligence Services (which of course includes Insikt Group!)

Levi Gundert

Chapter 1

The Case for Risk-Based Cybersecurity

Building a successful cybersecurity program isn't easy. One of the key factors is how you define success. In fact, if you define success the wrong way, you will end up with:

- A poor allocation of resources and time
- Misleading metrics that create the wrong incentives
- Grave failures of communication between security practitioners and management

That is exactly the situation where many cybersecurity organizations find themselves today. Their cybersecurity programs are either threat driven, focused on deploying industry best practice security controls to meet the latest cyber threats, or compliance driven, organized to "check the boxes" on security and privacy requirements produced by third-party standards organizations. Both of these approaches have grave flaws.

In this book, success is defined as a material and measurable reduction in operational risk. Adopting that definition of success will steer you towards processes and tools that lead to a better allocation of resources, meaningful metrics that drive the right incentives, and productive discussions between IT professionals, executives, and line managers.

> *Success is defined as a material and measurable reduction in operational risk.*

In this chapter and the next we will look at the differences between risk-driven, threat-driven, and compliance-driven cybersecurity programs. In the chapters that follow we will describe processes and tools for implementing risk-driven cybersecurity and best practices for managing some of its prerequisites (especially threat intelligence).

If you are an information security practitioner struggling to relate to your business, this book is for you. If you're an executive looking to make savvy security decisions based on strong risk metrics, this book is for you. This book will help you create a persistent information advantage for better security so your business can focus on being profitable.

Why You Should Listen to Me

Before we dive into these topics, I hope you'll allow me to indulge in a little reminiscing as I describe my background in the field. I don't want you to think I'm some guy on the street calling on you to upend your entire security strategy.

My first thoughts around the role that risk reduction plays in business strategies came when I was in university. I remember reading a book called "The Goal"[1] in an operations management class. The book's message — which is somewhat counterintuitive in our age of companies hyper-focused on revenue growth — is that profitability is the only meaningful business goal. For a business to thrive in perpetuity, every employee should be focused on that one bottom-line goal of increasing profits.

In the early 2000s, my work as a network security administrator gave me a front-row seat to many cyber events impacting operations at healthcare and financial services companies. Some analysts hypothesized that IT system interruptions were contributing to decreased productivity, resulting in lost revenue, but no one ever quantified the loss.

Fast-forward a few years. I was now sporting a badge and gun while pursuing cybercriminals around the world as a member of the United States Secret Service's electronic crimes task force. I quickly realized that the concept of cyber threat intelligence (CTI) was critical to criminal investigations, aiding in suspect attribution and successful prosecutions. My successful

---

1   Eliyahu M. Goldratt and Jeff Cox, *The Goal: A Process of Ongoing Improvement*: https://www.amazon.com/Goal-Process-Ongoing-Improvement/dp/0884271951/

cases started with proactive intelligence collection, almost always in coordination with brilliant minds in the private sector. I remember investigating the largest denial-of-service (DoS) attack at the time, and meeting Rabbi Rob Thomas, the CEO of Team Cymru (pronounced "cumree"), on the North American Network Operators Group (NANOG) mailing list. He was full of answers to the many questions I had.

It wasn't long before I rejoined the private sector (no more flying armed, but better data). Between consulting for clients and contributing to the defense of an enterprise, I realized that a specific articulation of risk was the greatest challenge facing senior cybersecurity leaders.

Risk Is the Language of Business

Cybersecurity professionals tend to see themselves as business enablers. As defenders, they keep the bad guys out so that the business can operate uninterrupted.

However, the C-suite and board of directors are more concerned with profitability. Often, those at the top of the organization see cybersecurity groups as cost centers dragging down the bottom line. Changing that cost center perception is critical to building a successful cybersecurity program.

Someone once said, "There should only be two types of people in a business — those who make things, and those who sell things." Today, there is a third category: those who defend things. This category is as necessary as the other two. However, while we have widely accepted procedures and metrics for measuring how people making things and people selling things contribute to the profitability of the enterprise (indeed, we have large accounting organizations set up to do exactly that), most organizations have barely started to think about how to measure the contribution of people who defend things.

How do you measure and communicate the value of a basic security control action? The answer lies in the language of risk. Senior decision-makers don't necessarily understand the language of security or even technology, but they speak the language of risk.

As a cybersecurity professional, your goal should be to quantify as a monetary value how every potential cybersecurity investment in staff and tools can reduce risk. If you can do that, you will find it much, much easier to:

- Set priorities among alternative cybersecurity investments, based on real outcomes for the enterprise
- Justify budget requests for each investment, and for the overall level of investment in cybersecurity
- Work productively with executives and line management to estimate risk and find the most cost-effective ways to reduce it

> *Quantify, as a monetary value, how every potential cybersecurity investment in staff and tools can reduce risk.*

Hard work and smart choices are required to achieve this goal, but it can be done. We will discuss many techniques throughout this book, but first, let's explore the problems that occur when you build your cybersecurity program around threats or compliance requirements.

Threat-Driven Security Programs

Threat-driven security programs implement industry best practice security controls based on the latest evolution of cyber threats. Little thought is given to whether a new category of threat poses a risk to the defender's business.

The distinction between threats and risks is extremely important. Threats are dangers — attacks that could potentially harm your organization. But not every cyber threat is a risk. If an existing control (process, technical, or otherwise) can defeat the threat, then it is not a risk for you.

> *Not every cyber threat is a risk. If an existing control can defeat the threat, then it is not a risk for you.*

For example, Hancitor (also known as Chanitor and TorDal) is a label for malicious code (malware) that acts as a Trojan capable of downloading additional Trojans. Hancitor is a payload typically delivered by email. When it first surfaced in 2014,[2] what made it worthy of attention was its ability to perform process hollowing: injecting code into a legitimate running process to disguise it from endpoint security software (like an antivirus client).

The author(s) of Hancitor innovated when they designed the code to install itself on victim machines as surreptitiously as possible.

If you weren't sure your endpoint security controls such as your antivirus software and endpoint detection and response (EDR) client were capable of detecting Hancitor's process hollowing, or you determined that there was a gap in your controls, then Hancitor posed a risk to your business.

However, if your endpoint security controls were capable of detecting process hollowing, then Hancitor was a threat, *but not a risk* for your organization.

Cybersecurity professionals should never take an action on a threat before understanding whether it represents a risk to the business. Why? Because the effort may waste valuable resources (time and money). The difference may seem academic, but the practical application of this philosophy is critical to a cybersecurity program's success.

Threat-driven security programs expend resources on threats that are not real risks (or are only minor risks) and miss opportunities to address serious threats. For example, security organizations that measure and reward teams for the number of threats mitigated create an incentive to work on threats that can be fixed quickly, even if they pose little risk, and to neglect complex and potentially more costly threats. IT managers who request funds to protect against the threats that are in the headlines, rather than issues that pose imminent risks to the enterprise, are more likely to suffer major data breaches.

2   Tweet, @jayTHL: https://twitter.com/JayTHL/status/527953029245325312

> *Threat-driven security programs expend resources on threats that are not real risks and miss opportunities to address serious threats.*

Compliance-Driven Security Programs

The goal of compliance-driven security programs is to increase maturity based on the criteria produced by a third-party standards organization. For example, ISO 27002 and the National Institute of Standards and Technology's (NIST) Cybersecurity Framework (CSF) are comprehensive compliance frameworks that periodically revise best practices guidance. Businesses following compliance-driven security programs rely on these third-party organizations to accurately identify threats and provide guidance on remediation actions for each category of threat.

These compliance frameworks are helpful guidelines, but ambiguity around emerging technologies and infrequent updates can leave gaps in their requirements.

Third-party compliance frameworks do encourage risk measurements, but they don't provide prescriptive guidance around how to actually measure risks. The best outcome when measuring and communicating value from a compliance-led cybersecurity program is announcing when a new maturity level is reached. However, not only is that metric subjective, it isn't a reliable indicator of risk.

Target Corporation is an often-cited textbook example of a devastating data breach suffered by an organization that measured very well on compliance.[3] In 2013 Target was certified as PCI (payment card industry) compliant. But the initial unauthorized access originated from a third-party heating, ventilation, and air conditioning (HVAC) vendor,[4] and at that time PCI compliance didn't require continual third-party access and risk auditing. Achieving compliance with the framework didn't prevent the breach.

---

3   TECHNEWSWORLD, *Target Breach Lesson: PCI Compliance Isn't Enough*: https://www.technewsworld.com/story/80160.html
4   BankInfo Security, *Target Vendor Acknowledges Breach*: https://www.bankinfosecurity.com/target-update-a-6489

Compliance-led security programs are dangerous for two reasons:

1. They produce a "check the box" mentality and encourage an attitude of fulfilling the letter of the law, but not the spirit.

2. Today businesses continuously introduce new technologies that increase complexity and risk, and the standards organizations can't keep pace.

Let's look at these two points in greater depth.

Following a compliance-based security program by just checking off a series of boxes may lead to complacency once a few best practices have been implemented. Governance and compliance obligations must be fulfilled, but compliance frameworks should be used as a tool, not the end goal or mission.

For example, if I tell you it's best practice to build a fence around your home to keep intruders out and you build a two-foot-high fence made out of pretzel sticks, you have fulfilled the letter of my request, but not the spirit. Are we just trying to keep rabbits out of the garden, or are we stopping thieves from breaking into the property?

If a governance or compliance framework (like COBIT, ISA, HIPAA, or PCI) mandates that you deploy stateful inspection firewalls, and you comply but mistakenly configure the rules to allow all incoming traffic, then you have satisfied the requirement but haven't reduced risk for the organization. Even worse, you have wasted resources on an ineffective solution.

If that same compliance framework requires a 24/7 security operations center (SOC) to manage alerts and you outsource the job to an incompetent vendor, then once again you've checked the box but made the organization worse off by both wasting resources and providing a false sense of security.

Moreover, when businesses adopt new technologies, they create new opportunities but also increase risk from cyber threats. New technologies add complexity to already complicated environments. Adversaries love complexity because it creates increased opportunities for attacks to succeed. More systems, more vendors, more suppliers, and less control of data mean the traditional security architecture playbooks must be revised to reflect a world where threats from third- and fourth-party integrations pose greater risks. Standards organizations simply can't move fast enough to address these new challenges, so their prescriptions will never cover all the new risks.

If you're not convinced that compliance frameworks fall short as an overarching goal, consider the increasingly dire news headlines around data breaches from 2016 to 2019. In 2016, Yahoo confirmed a data breach affecting 500 million customer accounts. In 2017, Equifax (one of three major American credit reporting agencies) sustained a data breach resulting in the theft of personally identifiable information (PII) from roughly 150 million American citizens. In 2018 Starwood Hotels & Resorts announced that they had been victimized for years, leading to the theft of the personally identifiable information of around 500 million guests.

Chapter 2

Risk and Risk Estimation

The Meaning of Risk

Presenting to a large cybersecurity audience on the topic of risk is hilarious. I can see the panic in people's eyes as they read the presentation agenda slide. The panic quickly gives way to resigned acceptance, followed by boredom and fatigue. Merely mentioning the word "risk" is like shining a bright flashing neon sign that says "Take out your personal device now and start perusing social media."

I've learned it's always best to engage the audience early, especially when presenting on risk. I start by asking the audience for a definition of risk. I never see more than one or two hands in a room of 100 people. The answers vary, but the constant theme is "damage" or "harm" — harm to a brand, damage to information systems, damage to people, and so on.

These definitions are based on the ordinary day-to-day use of the word, but they are not nearly rigorous enough to be used as the basis of business decision-making.

Unfortunately, finding consensus on the definition of risk is very difficult. Risk is a loaded term for many in cybersecurity, and prior experiences tend to color the perception of this important concept. There are plenty of experts in risk outside of IT. For example, enterprises in regulated industries like financial services have robust governance, risk, and compliance (GRC) teams for calculating all kinds of risk. However,

Risk is a loaded term for many in cybersecurity, and prior experiences tend to color the perception of this important concept.

these teams don't apply the same analytical rigor to the operating risk from cyber threats, and rarely have cybersecurity teams tried to adopt their methods.

Where can we look for a definition of risk that will help us manage cybersecurity?

Technical bodies are not much help. In its Network and Information Security (NIS) Directive, Article 4, the European Union Agency for Cybersecurity (ENISA) defines risk as "any reasonably identifiable circumstance or event having a potential adverse effect on the security of network and information systems." That's an overly convoluted definition that is also partially misleading.

Instead, cybersecurity organizations should adopt the definition of risk used by almost every business manager and board of directors: the potential for monetary loss.

Risk in this context is the possibility that an event will eventually lead to reduced company profitability. A cyber event causing damage to a company's brand or reputation can be quantified. The key question is always: how much does a cyber event ultimately cost the business?

> *Risk in this context is the possibility that an event will eventually lead to reduced company profitability.*

This is a simple but powerful definition. For people who defend things, it means that every decision can be guided by the answers to three questions:

1. If we take no action, what is the risk (how much money are we likely to lose from data breaches, disrupted operations, loss of reputation, or something else)?

2. If we take the action, how much does it reduce the risk (how much less money are we likely to lose)?

3. What is the cost of the action?

When cybersecurity professionals answer these questions, they speak the language of business. They can remove the cost center label and show how they are increasing profits.

Their budget requests can be compared against the requests of manufacturing, engineering, marketing, sales, and every other department in the enterprise. They can communicate with executives and board members who may have little understanding of technology.

Cybersecurity groups can approach risk the same way insurance companies do. Those firms don't write policies without understanding the risks. They use actuarial tables to underwrite life, property, and casualty policies, and if applicants don't fall within an acceptable range on any number of variables, then the policies are denied. Enterprise executives should require the same type of analysis for their own security functions to better understand the potential for loss, and whether security control changes are required to reduce potential losses to acceptable levels.

But We Can't Estimate Risk in Cybersecurity (Can We?)

"That sounds wonderful," I hear you say, "but in cybersecurity it is simply not practical to evaluate risk in monetary terms. There is little or no historical data for the new threats we face every day. We could never construct a financial model to capture all the detail needed for those calculations. Even if we could, we don't have anywhere near the time or the staff to estimate risks and costs precisely."

I understand your concerns, but let me assure you that in cybersecurity it is practical to evaluate risk in monetary terms. The key tools are the systematic use of estimation, which I'll discuss here, and a practical framework for risk modeling, which I'll present in the next chapter.

The Power of Estimation

As Douglas Hubbard and Richard Seiersen point out in their seminal work, "How to Measure Anything in Cybersecurity Risk," everyone wants perfect historical data for modeling, but such data is not necessary to create a meaningful model.

Hubbard and Seiersen make a compelling case for estimation; that is, training the brain to more accurately estimate values and allowing for black swan-type events. In the exercises that Hubbard and Seiersen present, the goal is a 90% confidence interval (where the correct value falls somewhere in the estimate range nine out of 10 times). The estimator must be confident that the correct value falls in the range between a low and high value.

> *Everyone wants perfect historical data for modeling, but such data is not necessary to create a meaningful model.*

For example, unless you're a student of European history, you likely don't know the exact year that the Battle of Waterloo was fought. Without skipping ahead, think of a range that fits here. What's your best estimate? You likely know that Waterloo occurred in Europe and you may know that it involved Napoleon. When calculating a range for the Battle of Waterloo you might guess a low value of 1500 and a high value of 1900. History buffs may define a tighter range of 1700 to 1850. The Battle of Waterloo occurred in 1815. If that year falls within your range, you correctly completed the estimate exercise.

Similarly, you can build a cybersecurity risk model by estimating ranges of monetary loss due to different cybersecurity events. You don't need to know the exact loss, but rather a range of reasonable losses.

Estimation Training Is Important

Estimation exercises are important to train the brain to account for uncertainty and overconfidence. A minority of people tend to be under-confident in their knowledge; a majority of people have an issue with overconfidence when estimating ranges. Trained estimation can help fill the gaps of imperfect historical data, especially when combined with valid statistical approaches like Monte Carlo simulations, which I'll explain in a moment.

Bias in estimation is what must be acknowledged and adjusted for to create higher-quality risk model results. When my colleague Dr. Bill Ladd and I walk clients through trained estimation exercises, they are surprised and dismayed when their estimate ranges are incorrect for half or more of the first 10 trivia questions. Overconfidence causes them to supply too narrow a range. But after multiple rounds, participants learn to widen their ranges to accommodate their lack of confidence in an answer. It's fun to watch them begin to understand their bias and adjust accordingly.

When the exercises move from random trivia to impact and loss across threat categories, the participants are rightfully wary of creating an estimate range without deep thought and consideration about their knowledge of the threat and the state of the organization's internal security controls.

It's interesting to watch as participants factor in loss mitigation controls like cyber insurance. The deductible for a major loss event may be a million dollars, making senior executives feel comfortable capping their high-end estimate loss value at that amount, even if the insurance coverage hasn't been thoroughly tested industry-wide.

Monte Carlo Simulations

Have you heard the joke about the statistician who nearly drowned trying to cross a river? He was informed that the average depth was three feet, and was surprised to find a seven-foot drop in the middle.

A risk analysis needs to consider not only averages ("expected values" in the terminology of probability), but also unlikely but possible minimums and maximums. These include "perfect storm" scenarios, where two or more bad things happen in the same period. A business might be able to overcome a flood, and it might be able to recover from an earthquake, but could it survive a flood and an earthquake in the same year? If not, what is the best way to reduce the maximum possible loss to an acceptable level: build a levee, earthquake-proof the headquarters building, or just buy more insurance?

Questions like those can be answered using Monte Carlo simulations. These involve selecting one random value for each model input out of a specified range and calculating the resulting losses. The simulation can be repeated thousands (or millions) of times and the distribution of losses can be examined.

Monte Carlo simulations are practical and easy to implement. In some cases, they can be computed and updated in an Excel spreadsheet. In the next chapter, I'll explain how they can be used.

Chapter 3

The Threat Category Risk (TCR) Framework

Most Cybersecurity Frameworks Are Not Based on Risk

We mentioned earlier that one requirement for risk-driven cybersecurity is a practical framework for risk modeling. Unfortunately, the best-known cyber threat taxonomies and frameworks, the Diamond Model,[5] the MITRE ATT&CK Matrix,[6] and the Lockheed Martin Kill Chain,[7] although helpful tools, are oriented toward identifying and remediating threats, not risks.

As with compliance frameworks, the population of cyber threat models should never represent the end state goal of a security team. If a tool or framework is too convoluted and not practical to use, then consider building a framework that is better suited for the human resources available and the desired outcomes. Framework categories should be intuitive and segmented at a reasonable level of granularity. "Practical" is obviously a subjective characterization, but like Supreme Court Justice Stewart's test of what constitutes pornography, cybersecurity professionals should know it when they see it.

---

5 Sergio Caltagirone, Andrew Pendergast, and Christopher Betz, *The Diamond Model of Intrusion Analysis*: http://www.activeresponse.org/wp-content/uploads/2013/07/diamond.pdf
6 MITRE, *ATT&CKtm Enterprise Matrix web page*: https://attack.mitre.org/matrices/enterprise/
7 Lockheed Martin, *Gaining the Advantage: Applying Cyber Kill Chain® Methodology to Network Defense*: https://www.lockheedmartin.com/content/dam/lockheed-martin/rms/documents/cyber/Gaining_the_Advantage_Cyber_Kill_Chain.pdf

> *The population of cyber threat models should never represent the end state goal of a security team.*

For example, I've observed security teams that spend months mapping one threat group's tactics, techniques, and procedures to the ATT&CK framework. That exercise helped improve internal network hunting methodologies. However, the time spent mapping that one group created a deficit of understanding for the tactics, techniques, and procedures (TTPs) of hundreds of other threat actors. In other words, the time spent on overly granular mapping isn't worth the benefit, especially when human resources are limited.

Similarly, deliberating over whether an adversary technique falls into the Kill Chain's "Phase 3 — Delivery" or "Phase 4 — Exploitation" is counterproductive. What's important is surfacing technique(s) and assessing them against existing security controls.

The Diamond Model focuses on mapping adversary infrastructure and capabilities as they relate to a victim. This model is especially helpful when attempting to attribute malicious activities to adversaries. However, it's less helpful outside of the public sector, where attribution is the operational outcome.

Introducing the Threat Category Risk (TCR) Framework

The threat category risk (TCR) framework, built on Hubbard and Seiersen's work, is a practical, quantitative risk framework designed to clearly articulate the probability and amount of economic loss that an organization faces from cyber threats in a given year. This makes it an ideal framework to drive a risk-based security program.

The Threat Category Risk framework is a quantitative risk framework designed to clearly articulate the probability and amount of economic loss that an organization faces from cyber threats.

The approach is very simple. The TCR framework starts with a set of general threat categories. For each threat category, a team estimates:

- The "event risk," which is the probability the event will occur in the coming 12 months

- The probability that, if the event does occur, it will result in the loss of confidentiality or integrity (that is, the improper disclosure of information or the unauthorized modification of data or system behavior), or the loss of availability (that is, a system outage), or both.

- The upper and lower bound of damage if a loss of confidentiality or integrity occurs

- The upper and lower bound of the duration (in hours), and the upper and lower bound of the cost per hour if a loss of availability occurs

Based on these estimates, a relatively simple calculation will reveal not only the most likely loss, but also a range of possible losses from the threat category.

We will walk through an example of the calculation in a moment, but you can probably grasp already a couple of significant characteristics of the TCR framework:

1. It calculates risk in monetary terms.

2. A team with the right skills, knowledge, and training in estimation should be able to provide the inputs with a reasonable amount of accuracy (especially because several of them are ranges) in a reasonable amount of time.

The Threat Categories

The first step in using the TCR framework is to select the threat categories that are relevant to your enterprise.

The categories listed in the table below are general on purpose. For ease of use and simplicity, they are divided between initial compromise methods and post-compromise methods — sometimes called "left of boom" and "right of boom," respectively. As Benji Hutchinson explained: "Popularized in military circles during the months and years after 9/11, the phrase 'left of boom' refers to the moments before an explosion or attack — a period when you still have time to prepare and avert a crisis. Right of boom, by contrast, includes the chaotic and deadly moments after the explosion or attack."[8]

Initial Compromise (Left of Boom)	Post-Compromise (Right of Boom)
Social Engineering*	Denial of Service (DoS)
Credential or Key Reuse/ Stuffing/Brute Forcing	Theft of Employee or Customer Personally Identifiable Information (PII)
Misusing Open Ports/ Network Shares (Manual or Automated — Worms)	Theft of Proprietary Communications or Information
Web Application Vulnerabilities (Including Web Shells)	Access and Theft of Data from Connected Third Parties
Hardware Vulnerabilities	Blackmail/Extortion
Software Vulnerabilities	Destruction of Data or Systems Availability
Protocol Hijacking (BGP/DNS)	Removal of Confidence in Data Integrity
Physical Tampering	Financial Fraud

*Includes phishing, spear phishing, business email compromise, and mislabeling malicious files in P2P networks

Note that TCR avoids excessive granularity in attack types, because great precision in estimating impact and loss ranges is not necessary in this framework. That saves us a lot of time and effort, because we only need to estimate the probabilities and impacts for a few threat categories.

---

8   Benji Hutchinson, NEC Today, *Left of Boom – Defeating the Threat Among Us*: https://nectoday.com/left-of-boom-defeating-the-threat-among-us/

The primary difference between TCR and other frameworks is that the threat categories are aligned to monetary loss. TCR isn't an adversary-centric framework, like the Diamond Model, because that would be redundant — it's implied that an adversary is manually or programmatically launching attacks.

Also, we don't have to analyze every possible threat category. We can focus on those that directly cost the business money. Some adversary tactics are important to detect because they indirectly contribute to loss, but for the purpose of calculating potential economic losses, they are less relevant. TCR is concerned with the threat categories and the subsequent actions that cause the loss of confidentiality, integrity, and availability of systems and data.

Walking Through an Example: Credential Reuse

Let's walk through the process of making estimates for one threat category that affects Acme Corporation: credential or key reuse/stuffing/brute forcing (we'll call it "credential reuse" for short).

Credential reuse typically occurs when an attacker steals credentials during a data breach (or purchases them on the dark web), and tests them against many websites and social media accounts. Unfortunately, it is a very effective and inexpensive way to penetrate networks and gain access to both confidential data and IT resources.

So how would we go about estimating the risk of credential reuse? The following charts are based on Hubbard and Seiersen's work.

We start by estimating the likelihood that the event will occur within the next 12 months. For simplicity, the second tuple/column in the table below ("Event risk") is summarized as a percentage instead of a high/low range estimate, but when implementing this model it's worthwhile to create range estimates for event risk as well.

Risk Type	Event Risk	CI Only	AV Only	Both
Credential Reuse	100%	60%	30%	10%

If a threat category is relevant (the event risk is above zero), the next step is estimating, if the event occurs, how often it will affect confidentiality and integrity only (CI only), the availability of data only (AV only), or both. For example, if I'm estimating values for Acme Corporation, I might estimate that the credential reuse threat category will impact information confidence/integrity only 60% of the time, availability only 30% of the time, and both 10% of the time.

If data confidentiality/integrity are impacted by a threat category (row), then the CL Low and CL High columns must be populated with a low value estimate and a high value estimate of cumulative losses in the next 12 months. For the Acme example, I estimate that incidents involving credential reuse will cost no less than $1,000 and no more than $25,000 over the next 12 months.

Risk Type	Event Risk	CI Only	AV Only	Both	CI Low	CI High
Credential Reuse	100%	60%	30%	10%	$1,000	$25,000

I've also determined, for the purposes of this exercise, that credential reuse is a threat category that could impact both data confidentiality/integrity and data availability. Where data availability may be impacted, I must provide low and high value time estimates (columns "Time Low" and "Time High") that are again aggregated for an annual time period.

Risk Type	Event Risk	CI Only	AV Only	Both	CI Low	CI High	Time Low	Time High	AV Low CPH*	AV High CPH*
Credential Reuse	100%	60%	30%	10%	$1,000	$25,000	50.0	300.0	$100	$250

*Cost per Hour

Related to the credential reuse threat category, I estimate that my low boundary for the year is 50 hours of lost data availability, and my high boundary is 300 hours. To create these estimates I need to understand the basic capabilities of current credential reuse TTPs used by attackers, and any mitigation controls that are in place to defend against them. Lost data availability may come from attackers' activities like misconfiguring network and security devices, shutting down servers, or destroying hard drives via wiper malware.

Finally, the "AV Low CPH" and "AV High CPH" columns represent low and high dollar amount estimates for the cost per hour due to the unavailability of systems or information. For example, if critical applications are not available due to an attack on a key server, I might estimate that the company will lose between $100 and $250 per hour.

Here is how our matrix might look if I entered estimates for all of the threat types facing ACME Corporation on the spreadsheet.

Risk Type	Event Risk	CI Only	AV Only	Both	CI Low	CI High	Time Low	Time High	AV Low CPH	AV High CPH
Social Engineering	100%	80%	10%	10%	$ 20,000	$ 250,000	1,200.00	3,000.00	$ 100	$ 250
Credential Reuse/Stuffing/Brute Forcing	100%	60%	30%	10%	$ 1,000	$ 25,000	50.00	300.00	$ 100	$ 250
Web Application Vulnerabilities	50%	40%	30%	30%	$ 5,000	$ 500,000	24.00	120.00	$ 500	$ 100,000
Denial of Service	5%	0%	100%	0%	-	-	1.00	24.00	$ 70,000	$ 240,000
Internet Protocol Hijacking (DNS/BGP)	5%	10%	80%	10%	$ 100	$ 1,000,000	.50	72.00	$ 10,000	$ 250,000
Hardware Vulnerabilities	50%	10%	60%	30%	$ 1,000	$ 1,000,000	3.00	336.00	$ 500	$ 100,000
Software Vulnerabilities (not web related)	100%	0%	100%	0%	-	-	50.00	1,500.00	$ 100	$ 500
Physical Tampering	10%	0%	90%	10%	$ 100	$ 1,000,000	.25	168.00	$ 500	$ 50,000

Running the Monte Carlo Simulation

Now that I've input my estimates for each threat category, I can run a Monte Carlo simulation and output the resulting median values for each row (see page 23).

I might specify 100,000 simulations, but since increasing the simulation count doesn't alter the median value variation significantly, there's no reason you can't specify one million simulations if you're so inclined.

The simulation will give us insight into both:

- The expected value of the loss for each risk category

- Unlikely, but potentially catastrophic, outcomes we might want to guard against

The first column of this spreadsheet shows the probability that a certain loss or a greater one will occur. For example, if you look in the "Total Loss" column, you can see that there is a 50% probability that Acme will lose $2.3 million or more, and a 1% probability that it loses $31 million. Likewise, if you look in the "Credential Reuse: Total Loss" column, you will see that in 40% of the simulations Acme loses roughly $1.1M or more in the next year from that threat category.

Most organizations understand basic losses represented in the top half of the percentile chart. Looking at the 50% row and seeing that the "expected" total loss is around $2.3 million, management might feel quite comfortable with the status quo (especially since the cost of operating an incident response team to triage successful phishing incidents or commodity malware infections can easily cost north of $2M a year in employee compensation and technical tools).

However, we also need to consider the figures below the 50th percentile row, particularly those that document the probability of loss between 50% and 15% (shaded in the figure). These loss amounts should encourage conversation. An organization that would accept a 50% probability of a $2.3M annual loss may reject a 15% probability of losing $5M in the current year.

The advantages of the TCR framework include simplicity, transparency, minimal resource requirements (a spreadsheet), and practicality (one or two days to train estimators on the process of estimating ranges for their organization). Because the model inputs of estimated ranges of loss are clearly specified, they can be discussed and improved if better estimates become available.

An organization that would accept a 50% probability of a $2.3M annual loss may reject a 15% probability of losing $5M in the current year.

Probability of This Loss or Greater	Total CI Loss	Total AV Loss	Total Loss	Credential Reuse: Total Loss	Web Application Exploitation: Total Loss	Exploited Vulnerability: Total Loss	Phishing: Total Loss	Ransomware (Internal Workstations Only): Total Loss
95%	$48,932.98	$1,108,327.00	$1,251,663.00	$580,034.60	$0.00	$0.00	$217,901.40	$9,404.66
90%	$63,457.61	$1,242,980.00	$1,403,847.00	$657,155.40	$0.00	$0.00	$247,986.70	$14,276.62
85%	$75,957.43	$1,350,330.00	$1,522,604.00	$714,480.80	$0.00	$0.00	$270,497.70	$18,792.91
80%	$87,625.05	$1,444,638.00	$1,630,886.00	$763,884.80	$0.00	$0.00	$289,878.00	$23,510.41
75%	$99,539.46	$1,534,862.00	$1,734,583.00	$809,776.70	$0.00	$0.00	$307,783.70	$28,501.25
70%	$111,585.25	$1,625,478.00	$1,838,824.00	$852,792.00	$0.00	$0.00	$324,799.00	$33,866.94
65%	$124,293.34	$1,719,219.00	$1,945,519.00	$894,525.00	$0.00	$0.00	$341,176.70	$39,657.47
60%	$137,632.16	$1,817,014.00	$2,059,930.00	$935,650.50	$0.00	$0.00	$357,726.00	$45,961.65
55%	$152,428.25	$1,924,844.00	$2,182,548.00	$977,639.10	$0.00	$0.00	$374,549.50	$53,213.17
50%	$168,940.79	$2,044,278.00	$2,320,317.00	$1,020,942.60	$14,674.47	$0.00	$391,791.10	$61,335.51
45%	$187,401.55	$2,181,988.00	$2,477,782.00	$1,064,832.10	$101,975.60	$45,128.89	$409,867.10	$70,839.06
40%	$209,070.60	$2,341,963.00	$2,666,050.00	$1,113,015.90	$174,960.29	$93,787.96	$429,149.10	$82,037.47
35%	$234,614.25	$2,538,985.00	$2,892,137.00	$1,165,631.10	$260,710.40	$160,561.43	$449,759.60	$95,359.09
30%	$266,081.91	$2,794,515.00	$3,178,194.00	$1,223,398.50	$373,392.09	$254,378.97	$473,006.80	$111,632.72
25%	$306,010.38	$3,136,882.00	$3,570,372.00	$1,288,149.30	$524,224.21	$395,223.73	$499,291.50	$132,252.68
20%	$361,115.69	$3,633,943.00	$4,110,297.00	$1,363,878.70	$747,733.01	$616,575.30	$530,187.90	$160,353.11
15%	$442,934.33	$4,425,370.00	$4,966,129.00	$1,459,628.40	$1,094,014.58	$1,010,318.04	$569,239.00	$200,229.88
10%	$586,292.40	$5,885,030.00	$6,496,379.00	$1,589,005.90	$1,754,853.29	$1,828,368.38	$622,563.20	$265,061.73
5%	$948,516.43	$9,657,421.00	$10,436,777.00	$1,801,617.20	$3,451,042.16	$4,297,746.59	$710,808.00	$401,099.91
1%	$2,984,718.46	$29,677,965.00	$31,056,102.00	$2,289,354.70	$11,883,288.27	$20,592,835.66	$918,448.80	$871,851.70

Estimating the Value of New Security Controls

In addition to estimating the probability of loss, the TCR framework enables security practitioners to estimate the value of implementing new security controls. Based on the expected improvements in security from the new controls, they can change inputs for the probability of event occurrences and the range of losses. They can then generate a new set of probable losses, calculate the delta, and compare the projected savings with the cost of the controls. The result is a dollar figure that can be shared with executives and bean counters alike, using their own language to justify the investment.

Consistent Communications

The anecdotal and qualitative approaches that many organizations use to measure and communicate security actions may be tempting for convenience and flexibility, but security practitioners risk alienating the business over time with potential message inconsistencies and misconceptions about risk. A logical and practical approach to quantifying risk, like the TCR framework, provides consistency and transparency in the measurement and communication of the value of security actions.

Control Validation

One additional method for consistently communicating security control improvements is control validation platforms. These are iterative approaches to testing security controls against realistic attacks such as red team exercises. Control validation is a beneficial tool for communicating security changes. It can complement quantitative risk scoring and sometimes even replace it in cases when security teams aren't ready to fully embrace TCR or other quantitative risk frameworks.

Chapter 4

Updating the Framework: RTDs and Threat Intelligence

Relevant Threat Deltas (RTDs)

n the previous chapter we introduced the Threat Category Risk (TCR) framework and discussed how to create an initial model for your organization. But once you have your model, when and how do you update it?

You might think the estimates need to be updated frequently. After all, cyberattacks occur every week, if not every day (or even every minute — have a look at a live perimeter firewall log). However, basic security controls will obviate the impact of attacks on most businesses, and truly innovative new threats are rare. Adversary technical innovation is largely opportunistic, and the pool of adversaries with advanced skills and an ability to innovate is relatively small when compared to the total pool of actors who are active in the underground economy.

However, you do need to update your TCR model when what I call a "relevant threat delta" (RTD) occurs. RTDs are caused by:

- New or modified threats sufficiently innovative to evade existing controls

- Changes to the organization's business or technology that expose it to threats that were not previously relevant

In other words, RTDs are events that change risks enough to have a material impact on your TCR model.

In practice, RTDs are infrequent enough so that TCR frameworks only need to be updated quarterly, bi-annually, or even annually.

That being said, you must be vigilant to ensure that you do discover RTDs in a timely manner. Businesses that don't make quick security control adjustments in response to changing threats are at increased risk of monetary loss. When a new RTD is discovered, there is a gap between the new threat and a business's security control response (which may include an information security vendor's updated response). Eventually the business or related security vendor will catch up, but businesses must be wary about those windows of adversarial opportunity.

> *Relevant Threat Deltas are events that change risks enough to have a material impact on your Threat Category Risk model.*

Why Threat Intelligence Is Critical for Risk-Based Cybersecurity

If RTDs initiate changes to your TCR framework, which drives your cybersecurity program, then several questions follow:

- How do you discover RTDs in a timely manner?

- How do you separate *relevant* threat deltas from *minor* threat deltas and *relevant-for-others-but-don't-affect-my-organization* threat deltas?

- How do you know how much to adjust your risk estimates when you verify that an RTD has occurred?

- Perhaps most important, how do you find the best options for improving security controls to minimize the impact on your security posture?

The answer to these questions is: threat intelligence, especially strategic threat intelligence.

Threat intelligence gives you visibility into the threat environment, including information about active adversaries and their TTPs. It enables you to discover RTDs early, sometimes in the planning or development stage, before attack campaigns are launched.

> *Threat intelligence gives you visibility into the threat environment and enables you to discover relevant threat deltas early.*

Also, by comparing adversary TTPs against your existing security controls, you can make informed judgments about what threats are relevant and material to your organization, the potential effects on your risk profile, and possible countermeasures.

The diagram below illustrates how to keep your TCR framework up to date.

1) Threat Intelligence → Relevant Threat Deltas

Define cyber threat categories and identify the threat events that change the risk model inputs.

2) Trained Estimation

Address the human bias toward over confidence before estimating ranges (lower / upper bounds).

The largest hurdle to implementing a quantitative risk model is internal acceptance and adoption.

Move beyond traffic light categories to specific probabilities for impact and associated dollar loss.

4) Review → Communicate → Advise

3) Monte Carlo Simulations

The process has four steps:

1. Threat intelligence allows you to identify threat events that change your inputs to the TCR risk model (the RTDs).

2. Your estimators use descriptions of the RTDs and related threat intelligence to update their probabilities and estimates.

3. Your rerun the Monte Carlo simulations with the revised inputs to produce new monetary estimates of risks.

4. The outputs of the Monte Carlo simulations allow business managers and cybersecurity professionals to work together to make decisions about acceptable risks and changes to security controls.

Chapter 5

Strategic Threat Intelligence

The Value of Threat Intelligence

As we mentioned in the previous chapter, threat intelligence enables businesses to identify adversary tactics, techniques, and procedures (TTPs) and determine whether new TTP instances will render existing security controls insufficient. Threat intelligence, via RTDs, should drive risk score changes, or measurably improve operational security, or do both.

This chapter addresses the ingredients of a good threat intelligence program, and the direct benefit to the business in tangible terms that demonstrate decreasing operational risk of economic loss through better security.

What Is Threat Intelligence?

It's clear that cyber threat intelligence constitutes a significant and growing chunk of business security budgets. As one indication, a recent survey found that 85% of IT organizations are currently using a threat intelligence service or planned to start using one within 12 months.[9] So what, exactly, is cyber threat intelligence?

My definition of intelligence is the act of formulating an analysis based on the identification, collection, and enrichment of relevant information.

Analysis is the key. It is the bridge between information and

9   CyberEdge Group, *2019 Cyberthreat Defense Report*: https://go.recordedfuture.com/cyberedge-cyberthreat-defense-report-2019

intelligence. Analysis is only accomplished through the separate and combined effort of the left and right sides of a human brain (and/or well-trained machines). The process and result of intelligence comes in many forms and applications.

In the professional world, intelligence is applied to a myriad of business problems, one of which is adversaries that seek to disrupt the confidentiality, integrity, and availability of information belonging to their victim(s). This is also known as a "threat." A practical definition of threat intelligence is defensive improvements created through analysis of the adversary's operating space.

The industry-recognized term is "cyber threat intelligence" (CTI). However, "security intelligence" is actually a more appropriate label, because successful threat intelligence is used across all of a security organization's various functions.

Recorded Future defines security intelligence as: "Intelligence employed across all security efforts to accelerate risk reduction exponentially."[10] Organizations give themselves a significant advantage by applying security intelligence to their threat prevention, third-party risk management, brand protection, security and incident response, vulnerability management, and geopolitical and physical security initiatives.

Recorded Future defines security intelligence as: "Intelligence employed across all security efforts to accelerate risk reduction exponentially."

Security intelligence provides an information advantage to connected enterprises. Since the beginning of time, humans have been seeking an edge. That pursuit has evolved through history. Today we all seek an information advantage in our daily lives — in sports, in traffic on our way to work, when shopping for a new car or buying groceries. How momentarily excited are you when your phone suggests an alternate route to work that saves you 10 minutes or you discover a website selling the same product for $50 less?

---

10 Recorded Future website: https://www.recordedfuture.com/security-intelligence/

Threat Intelligence Leads to Persistent Information Advantage

Threat intelligence allows organizations to anticipate risks and either head them off or react before they cause much damage. It also gives enterprises and law enforcement a shot at attributing attacks to their perpetrators, which changes the odds of catching the bad guys.

> *Threat intelligence allows organizations to anticipate risks and either head them off or react before they cause much damage.*

Early in my career with the U.S. Secret Service, I remember picking up my desk phone and taking a report from a man who explained how his mother had been victimized by a Nigerian email scam to the tune of half a million dollars. Naturally, this man was upset, and I felt terrible for him and his mother. Sadly, the likelihood of recovering funds at that time was slim to none, and slim was walking out the door. I quickly realized that threat intelligence was necessary to develop quality criminal leads that proactively generated cases before a victim picked up the phone.

Without threat intelligence and significant resources to pursue attribution, it's difficult to solve a cybercrime case. The biggest cases take years to prosecute. For the good guys, it feels like a game of whack-a-mole, with new criminals springing up quicker than the old ones can be nailed.

Start by Strengthening Basic Security Controls

Basic security controls are a good litmus test for more-advanced security measures like threat intelligence programs, just as door locks and a knowledge of where doors and windows are located are prerequisites for a home security system.

For instance, before the SOC and IR functions can work effectively, it is necessary to generate, collect, and analyze comprehensive host and network-based logs. Collecting breached credentials from criminal forums and automating the process of password resets are examples of valuable new security controls, but from a basic risk perspective, priority should be given to addressing shortcomings in password complexity and storage requirements.

Don't Rely on Daily Threat Reports

I have found that threat intelligence leaders often make the mistake of hiring analysts to create daily threat reports to increase awareness of threats throughout the business. In my experience, that's rarely a goal worthy of the budget necessary to create the capability.

A few years back, I was on site with a Fortune 500 client and asked about their threat intelligence program goals and the associated deliverables. The answer to both questions was a daily threat report. I asked how the reports created operational outcomes and how those outcomes were measured and communicated. I received a room full of shrugs.

That's about the time that I registered a small explosion in my brain. These were talented and motivated analysts working for a premier global enterprise, but their role had been reduced to second-hand reporting for the purpose of increasing awareness. I wanted to rewrite their mandate and charter on the spot, but of course that was beyond my control.

Daily Threat Reports Versus Useful Reports

Here's the difference between a topical daily threat report and a less periodic, more extensive report that includes assessment details.

A **daily threat report** is typically a short bulleted list of facts obtained from threat databases, together with associated impact ratings. A section might look like this:

- GandCrab Operators Resurface With REvil Malware (impact: low)
- Apple Zero-Day Vulnerability Exploited in New Bitpaymer Campaign (impact: low)

- Fancy Bear Returns with New Variant on Zebrocy Malware (impact: medium)
- Emotet Botnet Has New Template (impact: medium)
- Winnti Group Uses New Skip-2.0 Backdoor to Access MSSQL Servers (impact: high)
- NordVPN Confirms Data Breach (impact: low)

A **useful threat report** contains more valuable in-depth analysis that drives operational outcomes, such as:

- On November 1, 2019, CeleryStalk — an automated tool for network scanning and enumeration — was open sourced. The red team initiated external scanning of our enterprise environment with CeleryStalk which revealed two web servers with previously unknown PHP file and directory enumeration vulnerabilities that could lead to web shell implant(s) activity. Ticket #000001 containing specific guidance on remediating the affected web servers was opened with the IT admin group.

- On October 31, 2019, we identified new open source ransomware, labeled "Ransomware.PY" by the GitHub user cy4nguy. We tested the ransomware and verified its efficacy on both Windows 7 and Windows 10. Our current EDR software disabled this ransomware variant before it could fully execute. We will continue to monitor code updates and review our associated EDR detection as necessary.

- On October 10, 2019, we identified a newly registered domain with lexical similarity to one of our brands. On October 25, 2019 we observed the creation of a new DNS A record resolving to the typosquat domain. Additionally, on October 25, 2019, the typosquat domain's associated web server began using a self-signed SSL certificate. On November 1, 2019 we issued a domain takedown request with a third-party service.

- Between October 10 and October 28, 2019, we identified five new compromised employee credentials. We generated Active Directory password resets for the affected employee accounts.

- On October 12, Validolik (a member of the Russian-speaking Exploit forum) began selling over 100 web injects plus technical support for implementation in popular Android malware like Loki and Mazar. Our customer website is included in the list of web injects. We assess that our current malware detection software will sufficiently detect suspicious customer transactions likely initiated from Android devices compromised by Loki and Mazar.

The difference between the content in these two example reports is stark. The first report contains references to events that have been previously reported elsewhere. The impact estimates it provides are based on guesswork; its categorizations might give readers a general sense of the risk, but offer little rigor behind designations like "high/medium/low" or color terms like "red" and "amber." As a reader, should you lose more sleep over a "medium" or an "amber" designation?

Conversely, the second report contains first-party, original reporting on new events. Those events are accompanied by thorough assessments within the context of existing security controls. Further, each bullet reports remediation status and actions leading toward a final disposition that would ameliorate risk. The second report specifies outcomes that are measurable and communicates them in language a business manager would understand.

To create the second type of report you need both talented people and the proper tools. Even with adequate resources, certain assessment workflows require time. Given the frequency of daily threat events, it's next to impossible to provide a valuable daily threat report without enormous resources.

For these reasons, I recommend in no uncertain terms that executives should remove the daily report requirement and direct analysts to focus on quality reports issued weekly, monthly, or even quarterly. Quality trumps volume in private sector intelligence reporting.

Don't Create Reports for Nonexistent Audiences

Beyond occasional relevance for the public relations or legal department, threat reports that lack detailed security control assessments are in danger of serving a nonexistent audience. If you're building or managing a threat intelligence capability where the primary deliverable is reporting, you should ask yourself:

- Who reads these reports?
- How do the reports impact business decisions, particularly around security spending?
- What operational outcomes are occurring as a result of these reports?
- How do we measure and communicate the outcomes produced by reporting?

Stop Saying "Actionable"

There's a lot of confusion about what "actionable" means, although it's a popular word to throw around in meetings with executives. When I talk about threat intelligence with partners and clients, often they say, "I need intelligence that's actionable." That leaves it up to others in the room to interpret their intent, which usually produces very unexpected outcomes.

To be actionable, intelligence must have certain criteria that can be measured in consistent, unambiguous units understandable to the intended audience. That kind of intelligence can:

- Cause changes in our systems, processes, or workflows
- Be measured in concrete ways, for example by changes in risk levels, productivity, or costs
- Be communicated in a language that the audience understands, whether it is the rest of the security team, a manager, or an organization's board of directors

Risk-Based Analysis Helps Threat Intelligence

I said earlier that threat intelligence is essential to a risk-based security program because it enables you to discover RTDs and make informed judgments about what threats are relevant for your organization, the potential effects on your risk profile, and possible countermeasures.

But the reverse is also true: risk-based analysis like that provided by the TCR framework is needed to use security intelligence effectively. In addition, the threat intelligence group needs to obtain feedback on whether its output is understandable and useful.

In many organizations, threat intelligence reports are read by a few SOC analysts and executives. However, typically nothing happens because there is no risk-based analysis that justifies the required resources, and because the threat intelligence team never finds out why its output is ignored.

> *Risk-based analysis like that provided by the Threat Category Risk framework is needed to use security intelligence effectively.*

Let's say the threat intelligence team writes a report on the security merits of upgrading thousands of workstations from Windows 7 to Windows 10. The CIO and several direct reports read the report and decide that current cyber threats pose a risk to the Windows 7 status quo. The CIO recommends upgrading to Windows 10 and cites the threats listed by the threat intelligence team. However, the CFO makes a business decision to defer the upgrade with its million-dollar cost. In this scenario, the threat intelligence was valid but produced no operational outcomes.

If the threat intelligence team had used the TCR framework, it might have produced an analysis indicating that upgrading to Windows 10 would reduce risk by more than a million dollars in the first year. The analysis might even have shown that introducing additional security controls, or moving desktop processing to a cloud environment, would produce even greater reductions in risk and financial savings. In this case, the risk-based analysis would have pointed to positive operational outcomes and made the threat intelligence actionable for the organization.

For a second scenario, suppose a gaming company is thinking about moving operations from Las Vegas to Macau. The threat intelligence team writes a geopolitical risk report. The CEO reads the report but doesn't understand the implications of the findings, and so ignores key recommendations. Fortunately, the threat intelligence team has a process for capturing and communicating feedback from the CEO and other executives. The process makes them aware that their analysis was not framed in a way that was meaningful to non-technical management. Based on the feedback, they create a revised risk report that persuades the CEO and other managers to take key actions to enhance physical and digital security.

Should a business implement a cloud access security broker (CASB) solution? Should it invest in software to prevent executives from being victimized by a business email compromise (BEC)? Great questions, but it is difficult to prove the value of these solutions without monetary analysis and consistent feedback from executives. Increased awareness by itself is a goal with no outcomes, and by extension, it offers no value that can be measured and communicated.

Sourcing

A valuable threat intelligence program sets a goal of discovering RTDs and communicating them to the proper stakeholders. From that start, it works backward, via the intelligence lifecycle (which I will discuss in Chapter 10), to create the capability for delivering the kinds of reports that actually drive decisions. Part of this process involves specifying data collection and sourcing requirements, as well as applying the human skill sets necessary to maximize the data's value.

For each of the TCR threat categories in your model, you need to evaluate data requirements. There are six broad types of threat intelligence data:

1. Open source
2. Closed source

3. Passive telemetry
4. Active telemetry
5. Customer telemetry
6. Malware-processed metadata

It's important to understand each data type and how it's collected. It may be easier, save time, and limit legal risk to use vendors or other third parties for collecting specific types of data, and each threat category may require different data sets to fulfill the collection requirements.

Open source

The largest collection of open source data typically originates on the World Wide Web, but sources also include chat forums like Internet Relay Chat (IRC) networks, WhatsApp, and Telegram. If the data is discoverable and free to collect, then it's open source data. For example, although Tor sites (sites using a .onion TLD) are often lumped under the "dark web" label and assumed to count as closed sources, unless a Tor forum requires vetting or payment to participate, the data collected there is open source.

Closed source

Closed source data requires special access. The underlying data inhabits the same media as open source data — web, chat, and so on — but access must first be established. In the case of criminal forums, often a payment is required or members must vouch for the online moniker before access is granted. The marketing departments in a lot of cybersecurity organizations like to refer to this data as originating from the "dark web," but if vetting is required, then "closed source" is a more accurate description.

Passive telemetry

The best way to think about passive data collection (telemetry) is to visualize a sensor or network of sensors that log interactions with other devices. A good example is a honeypot (a computer that deceptively mimics services) or "dark" IP space (darknet) that has no legitimate purpose beyond interacting with or logging activity from internet (or internal network) hosts. These collect and log packets and files from rogue hosts (and only from rogue hosts, because legitimate hosts wouldn't be interacting with dark IP space or a honeypot). GreyNoise is an example of a commercial service for passive telemetry.

Active telemetry

Active telemetry involves scanning internet hosts and enumerating their ports, associated services, vulnerabilities, and so on. Shodan, Censys, and Binary Edge are classic examples of commercial services that actively crawl the internet and store the resulting data for customer querying.

Customer telemetry

Customer telemetry is the data produced by a customer's endpoints or network. That data is sent to an appliance or software owner. For example, Microsoft produces the world's most prolific software operating system - Windows. Hypothetically, if Windows collects basic system information (e.g. geographic locations where Windows is installed) and sends that data back to Microsoft, then Microsoft is generating customer telemetry, in part to help it improve its products. Customer telemetry is a rich source of information from large enterprises because of their access to and insights about global endpoints and networks.

Malware-processed metadata

Malware-processed metadata is its own threat intelligence data type because the number of malicious code (malware) samples is large. The exact number is impossible to pinpoint at any given time, but the volume is immense — somewhere on the order of yottabytes. Open source tools (such as Cuckoo Sandbox) and commercial ones (Joe Sandbox) detonate malicious code — that is, they execute files on an isolated computer or phone or in an emulated environment — and extract metadata about the actions of the malware file. The commercial services that store and analyze patterns in malware metadata are useful resources for establishing ground truth about a particular file. The best-known commercial services for malware metadata storage and searching are VirusTotal and ReversingLabs.

Staffing and Community Support

Strategic threat intelligence programs thrive when they are staffed by analysts with diverse skill sets.

Broadly speaking, I see analysts with three types of experience as contributing the most to threat intelligence programs:

- Military and intelligence backgrounds
- Law enforcement experience
- Technical backgrounds

Analysts from military and intelligence agencies understand the process of data collection, analysis, and reporting. They understand biases and seek clarity in their conclusions. There are private sector threat intelligence teams that dedicate whole teams of analysts to each of the intelligence lifecycle functions.

I've personally observed massive teams within financial services companies that likely rival the intelligence capabilities of small countries. They have large teams of analysts and engineers dedicated to intelligence collection, analysis, and reporting.

Law enforcement analysts and agents may be less familiar with the traditional intelligence lifecycle, but they have knowledge and experience about criminal tactics and methods and are accustomed to distinguishing fact from opinion.

Technical information security practitioners are critical to the successful production of threat intelligence because they have a deep background in one or several technical security disciplines such as security operations, incident response, security engineering and architecture, vulnerability management, and red teaming. Practitioners with a technical background are necessary for their deep knowledge of security controls and offensive tradecraft, and also because they understand specialties like malware reverse engineering, infrastructure design and maintenance, and network and host-based forensics.

Only a team with multiple types of human resources can produce high-quality strategic threat intelligence. Identifying RTDs requires intelligence analysts and technical engineers to work together to discover new cyber threats, assess their impact on existing security controls, and estimate the resulting change in risk.

It's important for CISOs to support their threat intelligence team's participation in conferences, events, email lists, Slack channels, IRC channels, and other spaces where security professionals network with each other and discuss common challenges and solutions. Because cyber threats evolve quickly, it's critical for threat intelligence professionals to have buy-in from team leaders to spend time and budget on physical and virtual participation in communities that will benefit the security group and ultimately the business.

These communities are vital to creative and effective solutions. A strategic threat intelligence practice with continuous input and feedback from peers in similar and dissimilar industries will have a more informed and more effective team.

A strategic threat intelligence practice with continuous input and feedback from peers in similar and dissimilar industries will have a more informed and more effective team.

Avoid Siloing

You need to consider the placement of the threat intelligence function within your larger security organization. Because threat intelligence is often the new kid on the block, long-term success is dictated by the reception it receives from other security teams. On multiple occasions, I've witnessed dysfunctional enterprise security teams whose members actually view threat intelligence as a threat due to perceived role and responsibility overlap. I've personally had team leaders in lateral security groups tell me (sometimes during my first week on the job) that they have zero interest in collaboration because they don't want to see their mission or span of control eroded.

The easiest route to continued security control improvement is to embed the threat intelligence team in a veteran group, such as incident response or security architecture/engineering, which has strong relationships in place with lateral security teams. This organizational structure will help alleviate counterproductive posturing and politics that get in the way of results.

I can't stress enough that effective security is a cross-functional, cooperative effort. Walls between groups, whether caused by lack of communication, workflows that don't overlap, or big egos, need to be eliminated. When different security functions are siloed, critical information and intelligence doesn't get shared with the people who would benefit the most from it. My colleagues and I have seen many situations where the security operations and incident response teams don't share "their" data with the threat intelligence team because they want to control where that data goes. This causes nothing but harm.

> *Walls between groups, whether caused by lack of communication, workflows that don't overlap, or big egos, need to be eliminated.*

Other teams often think that threat intelligence is produced only from external sources by a dedicated team. They forget that the most important threat intelligence, and the first that should be generated and considered, comes from incident response teams who have visibility into what's happening within their own organizational infrastructure. That's what you should care about the most — not some report on a new exploit being used by some foreign threat against some other industry.

Tooling and Measurements

The final step in creating a successful strategic threat intelligence capability is defining the tools and workflows necessary to maximize the value of threat data.

Simplicity is the most important principle here. Indicators of attack or compromise (IOAs and IOCs), most commonly IP addresses, domains, and file hashes, are important for immediate response to ongoing attacks, but it's adversary TTP identification that is necessary for exposing risk.

Generally, a database is required to store and share data. Something as simple as sharing EverNote/OneNote notebooks may be sufficient. Threat intelligence teams should avoid the trap of overthinking these tooling and workflow requirements. Spending years designing a threat intelligence database system to store analyst notes or IOCs and IOAs is a poor investment for any business.

Once the threat intelligence team is generating RTDs to feed threat category risk (TCR) inputs and to better communicate with senior stakeholders via the risk model output values, the next step is creating strong relationships with lateral security teams for improved security controls. This requires agreement upon communication channels and intelligence formatting so everyone can obtain and use threat data.

If the incident response team works with tickets created in a system of record like JIRA or ServiceNow, then the threat intelligence team should accommodate that existing workflow. Peer security groups like incident response, vulnerability management, fraud, threat hunting, and security engineering should regularly talk about recommendations for security control improvements that cover both technical aspects and policy decisions.

I previously discussed communicating risk to senior business leaders in terms of changes in the probability of loss. These changes are driven by RTDs, so it is important to track the quantity and quality of documented RTDs.

In fact, RTDs are the most important metric for the threat intelligence team. Measurements of RTDs inform the frequency of security control improvements generated by partner teams. Remember that security control improvements positively affect threat-category risk model inputs, whereas RTDs may affect them negatively (until a security control improvement is made). In simpler terms, the right security control inputs will create a narrower and more accurate range for risk assessment, while relevant threat deltas will do the opposite.

Don't waste time splitting hairs over whether something is a metric, a key performance indicator (KPI), or an objective and key result (OKR). Decide on terms and definitions that are acceptable to the business, and then begin consistently measuring.

Mean time to detect (MTtD) and mean time to resolve (MTtR) are common metrics for incident response teams, and they can also be adapted for threat intelligence. Specifically, you can measure the mean time to surface (MTtS) and the mean time to assess (MTtA) new threat actor TTPs. These are valuable metrics to show progress over time.

Don't waste time splitting hairs over whether something is a metric, a key performance indicator, or an objective and key result.

There are two primary outlets for new TTPs — offensive scenario creation and internal telemetry hunting.

Creating new offensive scenarios to test existing security controls may require collaboration with a red team if your organization supports one. Translating TTP instances into a proprietary security control validation platform (e.g. AttackIQ) will achieve a similar result.

The threat hunting team (or the hunting function within the security team) should also convert newly discovered TTP instances into search criteria to be deployed in a SIEM or other telemetry database(s) in order to surface previously undetected adversary activity inside the business network.

Chapter 6

Additional Considerations for Strategic Threat Intelligence

Three A's for Addressing New TTP Instances

Don't assume that your security vendors are testing their products against real-life attacks and building in defenses. To identify relevant threat deltas, you need an efficient and iterative workflow around TTP instances. It should focus on three phases (the "three A's"):

- Awareness
- Assessment
- Amelioration

Information from the six sourcing buckets previously mentioned can help you maintain awareness of new TTP instances. However, you must have broad data access and smart alerting logic.

Here's a concrete example. On October 17, 2019, a new tool to hack Amazon AWS was released.[11] Many organizations were never aware of this release event, so they had no possibility of assessing the tool. Broad and programmatic awareness of threat events is a sourcing requirement.

Assessment and amelioration depend on the knowledge and skills of your analysts. Once a potential new tool or TTP instance is identified, dissection of the associated offensive

11 GitHub, *Fully Automated Remote Hacking Tool for Amazon AWS*: https://github.com/haroonawanofficial/Amazon-AWS-Hack

methods and techniques begins. This should include an assessment of current security control responses. Often this assessment phase requires manual intervention to properly emulate a TTP chain or build and operate a tool.

In the case of the AWS hacking tool, the assessment required downloading the Linux script to a non-production machine and running it against company-owned AWS instances. Where the script identified vulnerabilities in company-managed AWS buckets, the IT organization could make architecture changes and update security tools with new rules to detect scans on AWS buckets from this type of tool.

Security Control Validation

Security control validation can be a very effective way to test whether new TTPs can penetrate existing security controls and increase risks for the enterprise. However, traditional third-party red team and penetration testing engagements leave gaps. Hiring an external group to test security controls on an annual or even quarterly basis may satisfy compliance requirements, but it's insufficient to address the complexity and changes enterprises experience daily. Also, when penetration testers aren't rigorous about tracking and trying new TTPs, the exercise becomes no more than a test of whether the SOC or the blue (defense) team recognizes the penetration tester's favored techniques.

Companies like Qualys and Tenable provide software that constantly scans internal systems for technical vulnerabilities. Similarly, companies like AttackIQ provide software that programmatically tests security controls against the latest adversary TTPs. This software enables iterative "wargaming" that mimics the speed at which adversaries adapt to defenses, and immediately identifies gaps in security controls.

Security control validation platforms provide a valuable source of information on new TTP instances. Also, CISOs can use security control validation scores to tell a consistent story about changing risk to the board of directors. In addition to charting progress against a compliance framework, these scores chart operational security improvements (or deteriorations) over time in a reliable way.

Of course, any metric is prone to tampering, and these scores can be manipulated to tell a better story. Security teams can game any system to make scores look better (or worse), just like the chief of police or the mayor of a major city may reclassify certain crimes from major to minor to create the appearance of a drop in major crimes. But you can minimize tampering if you set your risk-reduction goals from the start, choose consistent standards to measure the outcomes of any changes, and communicate those changes consistently to stakeholders.

Workflows and Outcomes

Workflows can boost (or hinder) both efficiency and effectiveness. You should examine your key workflows to make sure they are providing the outcomes you need. Also, because in 2020 organizations of all sizes are struggling with a dearth of qualified human resources, you should aggressively pursue opportunities to automate analyst workflows. Increased automation will not only increase the productivity of your analysts, it will also improve outcomes and the ability to communicate those outcomes.

> *You should examine your key workflows to make sure they are providing the outcomes you need.*

The following list of threat intelligence workflows is ordered from easiest to automate to more complex and requiring more resources to automate:

1. Detection of brand and domain abuse and intellectual property leaks
2. Exposure analysis, particularly of technology stacks and third-party vendors and suppliers
3. Enrichment of indicator of attack and indicator of compromise (IOA/IOC) data for SecOps
4. Reporting
5. TTP instance identification and assessment
6. Risk qualification

Let's look at the purpose and opportunities for automation of each of these workflows (except the second, which was discussed in the previous chapter).

Detection of Brand Abuse and Intellectual Property Leaks

Phishing and domain abuse often coincide, but not always. Domain abuse is concerned with identifying attempts to spoof an organization's domains via typosquatting (the creation of domains that are slightly different from those of well-known organizations and are often used for phishing attacks, scams, and the sale of counterfeit goods). A typosquatting domain doesn't immediately correlate to malicious behavior but should be monitored and proactively removed where possible. Suitable open source tools like dnstwist[12] offer options for generating comprehensive domain permutations toward subsequent domain registration matching.

Code repositories and paste bins also require monitoring. I know from experience that developers enjoy maintaining code repositories on public resources for convenience. I've even observed developers backing up their entire hard drive daily to public code repositories. But code may contain private access keys and sensitive proprietary content (today software is the most valuable asset of many companies). It's generally bad practice to sync proprietary code to publicly accessible code repositories on shared resources like BitBucket or GitHub. Monitoring for sensitive disclosures should extend beyond code repositories to the general web.

In both cases — domain typosquatting and IP leaks — the workflow is straightforward. Scanning domain registries and the web can be handled by machines, and then humans typically assess new results when they surface. The assessment and amelioration pieces are difficult to automate with complete fidelity.

Exposure Analysis

Exposure analysis involves detecting vulnerabilities in assets (such as servers, endpoints, and security devices) and weaknesses in security controls, gathering contextual information

12 GitHub, *dnstwist*: https://github.com/elceef/dnstwist

about the vulnerabilities and weaknesses, and using that information to identify corrective measures and prioritize remediation. It begins with understanding assets and their relationships in real time. The challenge is managing the complexity of third parties and the constant adoption of new technologies.

Security intelligence helps address these challenges. It can uncover data on vendors and suppliers, including evidence of past data breaches and existing vulnerabilities, and provide context to prioritize patches for vulnerabilities.

Enrichment

Exposure analysis can be very labor intensive, so there is always room for improved intelligence automation in tracking changes to third-party profiles and enriching technology vulnerability context. To save time, most enterprises outsource to system integrators (SI) the construction of systems that collect enrichment data from multiple data sources and combine it in a master record like ServiceNow.

For example, Qualys, Tenable, and Rapid 7 all provide varying levels of programmatic vulnerability assessments against discovered assets in the network. Those data results should then be combined with threat enrichment in a system of record. Similarly, threat enrichment for third parties should be stored in a system of record. Proper system integration automates routine discovery and data collection tasks so analysts can concentrate on the strategic work of judging the impact of technical vulnerabilities and deciding how to address security issues at vendors and suppliers.

To obtain a complete picture of enterprise exposure at all times, it is important to include data from a variety of sources, including passive and active telemetry and open and closed sources, for programmatic threat enrichment.

Reporting

I previously described why it is dangerous to make daily reporting the primary vehicle for communicating strategic threat intelligence. When the main goal is increasing awareness, follow-up action and communication are almost universally absent. Remember that the goal of cybersecurity is creating operational outcomes that can be measured and communicated. For executives, a quarterly metric like "number of threat reports produced" is meaningless.

As I previously noted, the exception to this rule is when operational outcomes can be summarized to inform business decisions, typically those linked to a budget. If an enterprise cybersecurity program is already investing in quantifying risk, then finished reporting is straightforward, because it can focus on justifying spending to close highlighted gaps in security controls.

> *The goal of cybersecurity is creating operational outcomes that can be measured and communicated. For executives, a quarterly metric like "number of threat reports produced" is meaningless.*

Periodic reports tracking the number of new adversary tools and TTP instances identified, assessed, and ameliorated (in concert with adjacent security teams) will provide insight into the value of the threat intelligence team's workflow, and the benefits to the business in terms of risk reduction.

You can automate reporting workflows using security orchestration, automation and response (SOAR) products. One common use case is creating real-time dashboard reporting. Automation can also speed up the process of adding data and context to reports so they can be used for decision-making.

TTP Instance Identification and Assessment

Strategic threat intelligence workflows involve identifying and assessing the latest iteration of TTP instances across risk categories. Most of a threat intelligence team's time should be dedicated to the TTP instance workflow, because this is where human brains are required and deliver the biggest return on investment.

For example, phishing, as a subcategory of social engineering, remains a primary methodology for initial unauthorized access. Identifying the evolutions in phishing campaigns is necessary to reduce risk.

In 2020, adversaries are using different attachment types to evade traditional email security controls, including embedded Microsoft Office macros, JavaScript, Visual Basic scripts, object linking and embedding (OLE) content, HTA (HTML executable) files, and more. Many of these files fetch additional base64 encoded scripts from external web servers.

Adversaries also use email links that route to spoofed websites with pass through authentication credential capture features.

In the case of business email compromise (BEC), executives are targeted with a legitimate-sounding request that involves moving money to a purportedly legitimate recipient. No technology is required for a successful attack beyond the ability to successfully place a few paragraphs of text in a target's inbox.

Thus social engineering and phishing represent a considerable risk to most organizations, even those with robust technical and process controls in place. Strategic threat intelligence workflows involve identifying and assessing the latest iteration of TTP instances across risk categories.

The part of the workflow focused on identifying TTP instances can be improved with technology, but the assessment piece requires time. In fact, it can involve very extensive activities.

Once new TTP instances are identified, they can feed red team scenarios, control validation software, and new internal threat hunting scenarios.

When a red team is available, new scenarios should be built using the latest TTP instance iterations. The blue team should be attempting to identify red team efforts. If a red team isn't available, security control scoring software like AttackIQ is an alternative way to build scenarios and test controls.

The remediation part of the TTP identification workflow often requires collaboration with a security engineering or architecture group, particularly when the gaps in security controls are large. For example, in the case of phishing, if security controls prove insufficient against a specific offensive scenario, then the remediation part of the workflow may include deploying new controls like improved email gateway inspection, new Active Directory Group Policy monitoring, and ongoing analysis of quarantined attachments.

Risk Quantification

In Chapter 3 I discussed how to use the TCR framework to quantify risks so your organization can better understand the value of operational security outcomes. You should set up a workflow to ensure that your risk quantification activities are carried out systematically and that no steps, including the creation and use of RTDs, are missed.

Attribution

Before moving on to Chapter 7, let's address the value of adversary attribution.

General adversary attribution can be helpful because motivation informs methodology. Knowing why someone is carrying out a cyberattack can help us better anticipate their targets and the means they will use to perform that attack. Knowing who is carrying out that attack helps us determine why. Understanding an adversary's motivation allows us to better anticipate the TTPs they may use in the future, the level of resources they have available, how persistent their attacks might be, whether their attacks are targeted or untargeted.

> *Knowing why someone is carrying out a cyberattack can help us better anticipate their targets and the means they will use to perform that attack.*

However, more granular threat actor attribution (like name, address, picture, and so on) is irrelevant to the security needs of private sector organizations (although government security teams may need more detailed attribution).

For example, being able to attribute an unauthorized intrusion to the Chinese Ministry of State Security (MSS) is helpful context for TTP analysis, but there is no benefit to obtaining more specific information such as the name of the individual hacker working for the ministry or the address of the office where he or she sits.

Chapter 7

Operational Threat Intelligence

What Is Operational Threat Intelligence, and Why Do I Need It?

Operational threat intelligence automates the collection and analysis of threat data that can be used to uncover and block ongoing cyberattacks and campaigns by threat actors. Where strategic threat intelligence is primarily focused on adversary TTPs, operational threat intelligence is concerned with processing IOAs and IOCs such as IP addresses, domains, uniform resource identifiers (URIs), and file hashes associated with attacks. Operational threat intelligence can also provide vulnerability enrichment and metadata about internal technology stacks and third-party exposures, which may lead to operational outcomes in the form of detection and blocking rule sets (think YARA or Snort).

I often advise small and midsize businesses and enterprises with fewer resources to start their threat intelligence program with operational threat intelligence. Strategic threat intelligence programs are worthwhile but require substantial resources (including time) to execute properly. Strategic and operational threat intelligence are complementary, but if you only have the resources for one type, operational threat intelligence delivers great bang for the buck.

Operational threat intelligence can alert enterprises to previously undetected malicious activity, especially when threat data from outside the organization is correlated with internal telemetry obtained from a SIEM solution or an analytics tool. Even when correlation is not automated, organizations can start doing it simply by making sure that log data is visible and readily available to security teams. Once correlation activities are producing alerts, developing comprehensive SOAR workflows can reduce "noise" and false positives.

Operational threat intelligence delivers great bang for the buck.

Sourcing valuable external indicators can be challenging: costly if you are using vendors and time-consuming if you build your own infrastructure. Spending extra time digging into sourcing is always a valuable investment because it allows you to import only those indicators that will provide value.

I'll note here that many people make a distinction between operational and tactical threat intelligence (I think they believe "tactical" sounds high speed). It's a categorization that's vague and not very helpful for understanding the different values threat intelligence provides. For our purposes, it's enough to understand threat intelligence through the two frameworks of strategic and operational.

Operational threat intelligence is enabled by machines and it should be programmatically applied to enhance existing security controls. For example, key indicators can be sent directly to firewalls, web proxies, or internal intrusion detection systems to produce alerts immediately. This type of integration is extremely valuable for small (one- or two-person) IT departments that need to automate their way to value.

Regardless of available resources for telemetry, the quickest path to value from operational threat intelligence is to funnel it directly to security controls such as firewalls, IDS/IPS, EDR, web proxies, and DNS RPZ that can use the information to recognize and block malicious activity.

Large-scale telemetry correlation should only be considered once internal log collection is sufficient and sustainable. If the internal telemetry isn't available, or is only partially available, then the value of operational threat intelligence can't be realized.

Good and Bad Indicators

When you use operational threat intelligence, it is very important to distinguish between good and bad indicators. In this context, "good" means helpful for identifying attacks and unlikely to generate false positives, and "bad" means useless for finding attacks and likely to generate false positives and cause other problems.

The rationale for acquiring malicious indicators is that adversaries reuse TTPs, including infrastructure. Some threat actors are careful never to reuse infrastructure, but in my experience, most of them, even at the nation-state level, are lazy. They reuse infrastructure, following the old adage, "If it ain't broke, don't fix it."

Let's look at an example of a good indicator. Security researchers discovered that the Cobalt Strike tool used by adversaries contains a profilable secure socket layer (SSL) certificate. A server on the internet hosting a Cobalt Strike certificate has very likely been used in a cyberattack or will be used in one in the future. IP addresses and corresponding domains for such servers would be very good IOAs. You would want to distribute them to network and host-based security tools so they could block all traffic from those servers.

> *Most threat actors, even at the nation-state level, are lazy. They reuse infrastructure, following the old adage, "If it ain't broke, don't fix it."*

An example of a bad indicator is the IP address corresponding to a botnet controller located on a shared hosting platform. On such a platform, 10,000 domains may resolve to a single shared server IP address. If you blacklist that shared server IP address (through DNS RPZ, a web proxy, a firewall, or something else), all the legitimate resources hosted on the same server will become unavailable to the enterprise — potentially disrupting the work of some employees and causing panic among others who will believe the internet is broken. You will also cause your security analysts triaging security alerts to waste time on false positives because the internal traffic destined for the "rogue IP address" is actually legitimate traffic heading for other websites on the same shared server.

Domains provide much higher-fidelity signals than IP addresses for blocking botnet controllers and produce fewer false positives.

Another example of a poor fidelity indicator is IP addresses and domains of websites that serve out malvertising. Adversaries inject rogue advertisements into advertising networks,[13] and those ads redirect site visitors to a malicious exploit kit landing page on a server controlled by the adversary. But it is useless to block a website where the rogue ad appeared, because that website is not malicious, and neither are the vast majority of ads displayed there. (However, it may be useful to block the website hosting the exploit kit landing page, if it can be identified.)

The value of indicators can also be evaluated based on periodicity. For how long is an indicator malicious? One hour? One day? One week? An indicator that is only good for an hour is not very useful.

Before jumping into an operational threat intelligence workflow, consider the goals and the measurements. The overarching goal must be to reduce risk, but again, the devil is in the details around how to measure and communicate the risk reduction.

Measurement

Operational threat intelligence workflows create a number of intuitive metrics. For example, let's say you have a workflow that:

- Programmatically imports lists of breached user credentials (username, email address, and password)
- Compares the breached credentials to existing user accounts in Active Directory

---

13 United States Senate Permanent Subcommittee on Investigations, *Online Advertising and Hidden Hazards to Consumer Activity*: https://www.hsgac.senate.gov/imo/media/doc/REPORT%20-%20Online%20Advertising%20&%20Hidden%20Hazards%20to%20Consumer%20Security%20&%20Date%20Privacy%20(May%2015%202014)1.pdf

- Determines which of your employees have been affected
- Automatically resets the passwords of those employees

The number of employee account resets per period is a meaningful metric to report to the business because you are materially lowering the risk of data breaches.

Another example is removing or shutting down typosquatting domains. This is an operational outcome that can be measured and communicated. You might set up an operational intelligence workflow to:

- Scan domain registry services and surface new domain registrations that are permutations of your domains
- Enrich the domain listings with WHOIS data, name-server identity, and SSL certificate data for each potentially malicious domain candidate
- Add a subset of those domains and the related data to incident response tickets
- Send the tickets to the legal department or a third-party domain takedown service

Identifying and taking down typosquatting domains is an operational outcome that is worth measuring.

A third example is importing malicious IP addresses, file hashes, and domains for blocking actions. It's straightforward to track and report on the number of blocks. However, correlation for detection is less straightforward. The numbers of alerts triggered and triaged aren't meaningful because many of them may be false positives. Rather, it's the final outcomes that are important to measure: metrics like the number of identified infections or the number of security control changes made based on those newly identified infections.

A fourth example involves technology exposure analysis (vulnerability management). When importing operational threat intelligence data for vulnerability workflows, you might want to measure the number of:

- Vulnerabilities whose severity scores were altered based on programmatic enrichment

- Vulnerabilities enriched with evidence of exploitation in the wild that affect remote code execution (RCE) on internet-accessible systems

- Vulnerabilities and associated exploits identified before an official NVD/CVE identifier is publicly issued

Using these metrics to change risk scores in the TCR model will lead to changing monetary loss values. Even if you're not sold on the value of quantifying and monetizing risk, these are still meaningful intelligence metrics to communicate to senior stakeholders.

Chapter 8

Five Critical Cyber-security Functions

Security Is Preventing Unauthorized Access

undamentally, security is about answering a single question: How do I give the right people access to the right systems for the right amount of time, while keeping the wrong people out? Preventing and detecting unauthorized access is a key objective of cybersecurity.

Based on my experience, five core focus areas are critical to reducing the risk of remote unauthorized access for a majority of organizations. This chapter will focus on exploring those five:

1. Identity and access management
2. Vulnerability management (technology exposures)
3. Third- and fourth-party risk (relationship exposures)
4. Email security
5. Web security

If resources are short, these are the categories to prioritize.

The Problem of Identity and Access Management

The greatest problem in internet security is identity. Today, the internet underpins global commerce, personal finance, media, and many more essential parts of the world's economies and cultures. In all of these areas, there is no trust without identity — and identity is extraordinarily difficult to verify on the internet. Circumventing online identity verification mechanisms over the past few decades has generated unimaginable wealth for threat actors.[14]

The security industry has made some progress with multi-factor authentication (relying on something you are or something you have in addition to something you know). Unfortunately, in 2020 passwords alone are still widely used for authentication. Biometric validation — authentication based on something you are, like your fingerprint, retina scan, and so on — is a substantial improvement, but the software built on top of biometric authentication will always be vulnerable to tampering. There will always be unanticipated methods to bypass the next generation of authentication tools.

Interviews with experienced criminals and analysis of campaigns by state-sponsored actors reveal credential reuse to be a preferred mechanism for gaining initial unauthorized access. All businesses are potential targets, because the supply of stolen credentials seems to be limitless. Criminals can easily obtain access to vast troves of personally identifiable information in criminal marketplaces. Naturally, stolen credentials of employees with the highest levels of system access (e.g. administrators authorized to access Active Directory Domain Controllers) represent the greatest threat to a business.

Recent examples of threat actors reusing stolen credentials to gain unauthorized access to corporate networks include:

- Visma, a Norwegian managed service provider, which was attacked by APT10, a nation-state sponsored threat actor, for the purposes of industrial surveillance (see the diagram below)

- Target, the American retailer, which suffered a substantial breach and data loss at the hands of criminals searching for opportunity

---

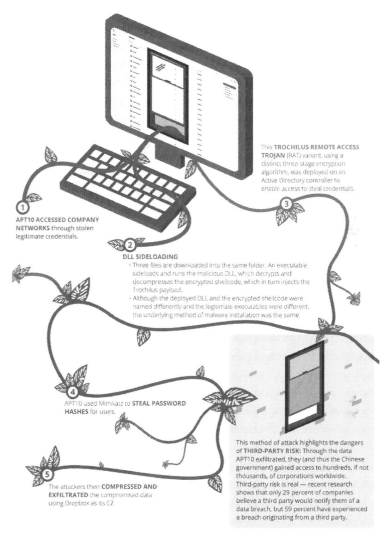

This **TROCHILUS REMOTE ACCESS TROJAN** (RAT) variant, using a distinct three-stage encryption algorithm, was deployed on an Active Directory controller to enable access to steal credentials.

1 APT10 ACCESSED COMPANY NETWORKS through stolen legitimate credentials.

2 DLL SIDELOADING
- Three files are downloaded into the same folder. An executable sideloads and runs the malicious DLL, which decrypts and decompresses the encrypted shellcode, which in turn injects the Trochilus payload.
- Although the deployed DLL and the encrypted shellcode were named differently and the legitimate executables were different, the underlying method of malware installation was the same.

4 APT10 used Mimikatz to **STEAL PASSWORD HASHES** for users.

5 The attackers then **COMPRESSED AND EXFILTRATED** the compromised data using Dropbox as its C2.

This method of attack highlights the dangers of **THIRD-PARTY RISK**: Through the data APT10 exfiltrated, they (and thus the Chinese government) gained access to hundreds, if not thousands, of corporations worldwide. Third-party risk is real — recent research shows that only 29 percent of companies believe a third party would notify them of a data breach, but 59 percent have experienced a breach originating from a third party.

The TTPs APT10 used to breach Visma's systems. (Source: Recorded Future)

These were not isolated incidents against small and unprepared organizations.

Abusing customer services for fraud and financial gain is also a popular activity in the underground economy. Due to the massive availability of stolen credentials obtained via breached databases, it's never been easier for adversaries to execute credential reuse.[15] This dynamic is possible because people are lazy — it's just much easier and more convenient to use one set of credentials to access multiple online resources.

IAM That IAM

Achieving comprehensive identity and access management (IAM) throughout an enterprise requires significant resources, including time, budget, and skilled security architecture and engineering groups.

The traditional challenge for CISOs is maintaining a patchwork of IAM solutions for various legacy systems and applications coupled with partial coverage for multi-factor solutions. The adoption of cloud and mobile technologies is rendering traditional network boundaries obsolete and putting further stress on the scalability of legacy IAM solutions. Cloud access security broker solutions have recently emerged in part to address the gap created when organizations attempt to extend IAM security policies to cloud resources.

Strategic threat intelligence is a force multiplier for the IAM function because it uncovers new adversary TTPs for bypassing authentication, authorization, tokenization, and other IAM functions.

For example, when pass-the-hash (PtH) attacks emerged in 2014, Microsoft issued remediative guidance suggesting actions that reduced risk.[16] But organizations that waited for Microsoft to issue formal recommendations were often too late. Rapid awareness and assessment were necessary to address architecture deficiencies prior to Microsoft's issuing of formal recommendations.

Strategic threat intelligence is a force multiplier for the identity and access management function because it uncovers new adversary TTPs for bypassing authentication, authorization, tokenization.

15 Insikt Group, *The Economy of Credential Stuffing Attacks*: https://www.recordedfuture.com/credential-stuffing-attacks/
16 Microsoft, *Mitigating Pass-the-Hash (PtH) Attacks and Other Credential Theft*: https://www.microsoft.com/en-us/download/details.aspx?id=36036

Similarly, obtaining organizational credentials from database breaches helps prevent customer account takeovers (ATO) and future credential reuse on the network.

Measuring and communicating the value of outcomes in IAM is relatively straightforward because senior stakeholders understand the basic concepts of identity and access.

The Role of Security Intelligence in Vulnerability Management

Organizations using vulnerability risk management (VRM) often struggle to properly identify vulnerability exposure and to apply patches and workarounds in a timely manner. Heterogenous and legacy environments for hardware and software, together with a lack of confidence about complete asset inventory, make vulnerability management an extremely resource-intensive activity.

Additionally, in enterprises with multiple lines of business, there is often a justifiable reluctance to patch when the possibility exists of prolonged outages of mission-critical systems. Business owners often prefer to accept the risk of unauthorized activity when the alternative is system downtime.

Operational threat intelligence can play a major role in VRM by:

- Turbocharging patching efforts
- Clarifying the value of vulnerability remediation activities to skeptical business units

Although most vulnerability management processes rely on the common vulnerability scoring system (CVSS),[17] vulnerability management teams need additional context beyond the CVSS base scores to increase severity scores where appropriate. That evidence may originate from internal asset data or threat intelligence articulation. As discussed in previous chapters, a good threat intelligence workflow automates the process of enriching data about vulnerabilities and feeding the information into a system of record like JIRA or ServiceNow.

---

17 NIST, *Vulnerability Metrics*: https://nvd.nist.gov/vuln-metrics/cvss

Threat intelligence in vulnerability management should be measured by the number of pre-CVE (common vulnerabilities and exposures)[18] vulnerabilities surfaced, and how often severity ratings are changed based on evidence of remote code execution (RCE) that could potentially affect internet-facing systems.

Third- and Fourth-Party Risk

Vulnerability management and third-party risk form one logical continuum. Both functions address surfacing and assessing exposures iteratively. While the VRM team addresses the potential for exposure in internal technology stacks, the governance, risk, and compliance (GRC) team focuses on external exposures via third parties, including potential exposures in their technology stacks.

It's understandable that adversaries see third-party relationships as natural avenues for exploitation. They can piggyback on pre-existing relationships between enterprises and their vendors, suppliers, and other trusted third parties. Digital supply chains continue to grow in scale and complexity, creating even more exposure for organizations that don't perform due diligence on their business partners or monitor them on an ongoing basis.

Examples abound of enterprises being compromised through trusted third parties. In late 2017, [24]7.ai — an online chat vendor — was compromised[19] and personally identifiable information (PII) was lost from many national retailers that had technical integrations with [24]7.ai. In early 2018, MyFitnessPal (an Under Armour business unit) was attacked and PII subsequently exfiltrated.[20] Universal Music Group[21]

18 CVE website: https://cve.mitre.org
19 Lee Mathews, Forbes, Hacked Chat Service Exposes Data From Best Buy, Sears, Kmart And Delta: https://www.forbes.com/sites/leemathews/2018/04/09/hacked-chat-service-exposes-data-from-best-buy-sears-kmart-and-delta/#3c0e9d8f3055
20 Alyssa Newcomb, Fortune, *Hacked MyFitnessPal Data Goes on Sale on the Dark Web — One Year After the Breach*: https://fortune.com/2019/02/14/hacked-myfitnesspal-data-sale-dark-web-one-year-breach/
21 Tara Seals, threatpost, *Honda, Universal Music Group Expose Sensitive Data in Misconfig Blunders*: https://threatpost.com/honda-universal-music-group-expose-sensitive-data-in-misconfig-blunders/132451/

and MyHeritage[22] experienced similar victimization via vendor relationships.

Managing third- and fourth-party (the vendors' vendors) exposure begins with tiering organizations by the level of access permitted to the primary enterprise. It isn't as critical to oversee the office supply company restocking printer paper as it is to monitor the online human resources and payroll service provider.

Organizations should create and maintain a list of third parties with access to customer or proprietary systems and data. The list should be segmented by the time and level of access required. In an enterprise this task is typically the responsibility of a GRC group. That group should use a system of record to track updates and changes to the status of third-party relationships, as well as their compliance with security policies such as patching known vulnerabilities.

You can accomplish even more by applying a security intelligence philosophy to other aspects of third-party risk, and by integrating operational threat intelligence into the existing third-party system of record.

Let's say your organization has a relationship with "ABC Corp," a company that provides online payment transaction services. While you have an interest in ABC's long term economic viability, its current cybersecurity disposition is even more important. You should use threat intelligence and vulnerability scans to monitor:

- Exposed credentials (including email addresses and API keys) in open and closed web sources
- ABC's use of website technology versions known to have vulnerabilities
- Previous breach disclosures
- Evidence of commodity network infections
  Past and current infrastructure misconfigurations
- Unattended domain typosquatting

When new events occur in the categories above, an audit of

---

22 Kristen V Brown, Bloomberg, *Hack of DNA Website Exposes Data From 92 Million Accounts*: https://www.bloomberg.com/news/articles/2018-06-05/hack-of-dna-website-exposes-data-from-92-million-user-accounts

the third party in question may be warranted. GRC needs the authority to initiate audits. If those audits fail, then GRC needs the power to terminate the vendor or supplier relationship. Culturally, this can be a difficult recommendation, especially if the third party is integral to business operations, but leaving the relationship intact may increase financial loss in the event of a data breach.

Email and Web Security

Access to email and the web are non-negotiable capabilities for most employees, and a web presence is necessary for even the least technology-savvy organization. Unfortunately, both email and web services are primary attack vectors. Phishing remains stubbornly effective. The best technical controls, like email security gateways, won't prevent a persistent adversary from successfully phishing employees, primarily because phishers continue to discover new methodologies for bypassing even the latest security gateway techniques like detailed content inspection, domain history, and sender policy framework (SPF).

That doesn't mean email security gateways are ineffective — quite the opposite. But even a 0.005% success rate for a phishing campaign can mean serious damage for the enterprise.

A few high-profile organizations whose attacks began with phishing include the Democratic National Committee,[23] Sony Pictures,[24] and Xoom.[25]

Likewise, opportunistic drive-by download attacks (or targeted "watering holes"),[26] coupled with malvertising,[27] create another scenario for persistent attacks. Just as email security

---

23 Philip Bump, The Washington Post, *Timeline: How Russian agents allegedly hacked the DNC and Clinton's campaign*: https://www.washingtonpost.com/news/politics/wp/2018/07/13/timeline-how-russian-agents-allegedly-hacked-the-dnc-and-clintons-campaign/

24 Edgar Alvarez, engadget, *Sony Pictures hack: the whole story*: https://www.engadget.com/2014/12/10/sony-pictures-hack-the-whole-story/

25 Therese Poletti, MarketWatch, *The strange case of a money-transfer firm's missing millions*: https://www.marketwatch.com/story/the-strange-case-of-a-money-transfer-firms-missing-millions-2015-01-07

26 Levi Gundert et al., Cisco blogs, *Fiesta Exploit Pack is No Party for Drive-By Victims*: https://blogs.cisco.com/security/fiesta-exploit-pack-is-no-party-for-drive-by-victims

27 Levi Gundert et al., *Cisco blogs, Angling for Silverlight Exploits*: https://blogs.cisco.com/security/angling-for-silverlight-exploits

gateways are designed to address spam and phishing, properly configured DNS RPZs (response policy zones)[28] and web proxies are designed to detect and block traffic to rogue web destinations. Consistent client machine patching also mitigates the risk from most drive-by attacks. However, the web servers that organizations own and manage present their own unique security challenges.

Web shells are another serious risk — in my experience perhaps the most misunderstood and overlooked operational risk to modern enterprises. A web shell is code that is interpreted and run by an HTTP server daemon (a "web server") and in most cases is designed to provide a graphical interface for remote access to the server, its file system, and often the underlying operating system. Web shells aren't inherently malicious, but most web shell code is created and maintained by adversaries.

Web shells don't magically appear on servers. Rather, adversaries typically identify an exploitable vulnerability on a web server, then upload their web shell file to a writable directory or modify an existing file. Even the most technically challenged adversaries can locate vulnerable web servers in minutes through open source information and dorking.[29] Once the web shell is accessible, the threat actor can use it for an array of malicious activities, including:

- Searching for credentials
- Defacing web pages
- Elevating privileges
- Identifying additional resources on the target network
- Locating databases and exfiltrating data
- Launching denial of service attacks
- Redirecting website visitors to watering hole and drive-by campaigns
- Installing a proxy for future anonymization
- Maintaining long-term persistence on the server

28 DNS Response Policy Zones website: https://dnsrpz.info
29 Wikipedia, Google hacking: https://en.wikipedia.org/wiki/Google_hacking

There are no silver bullets for phishing and web shell detection, but a winning recipe is a multi-pronged strategy that includes:

- Continuous infrastructure awareness
- Server hardening
- Aggressive threat hunting[30]

Operational threat intelligence can play an important part in this multi-pronged strategy. For example, threat intelligence can provide:

- IP addresses and domains of servers and bots on the internet associated with spam and phishing campaigns
- "Chatter" on dark web forums about planned phishing campaigns
- Discussions about vulnerabilities on web servers that can be exploited by web shells (and sometimes even lists of IP addresses of servers with those vulnerabilities)
- TTPs used in phishing and web shell-based attacks

Organizations can use this information to shut down some attacks immediately, for example by blocking network traffic from external web sites used in these attacks.

In addition, threat intelligence can help build playbooks for threat hunters. The art of threat hunting is identifying patterns and anomalies in telemetry (log data) that are likely indicators of malicious activity. A friend of mine describes the practice as dumpster diving — there's a lot of trash to search through to discover something useful. Threat intelligence can give threat hunters insights into what indicators and artifacts on networks, servers, and endpoints will reveal about the presence of attacks based on phishing and web shells.

---

30 Jeff Bollinger, Brandon Enright, Matthew Valites, *Crafting the InfoSec Playbook: Security Monitoring and Incident Response Master Plan*: https://www.amazon.com/Crafting-InfoSec-Playbook-Security-Monitoring/dp/1491949406

Chapter 9

Happy Humans: The Most Important Ingredient

any technological solutions are essential to reducing risk, but security is really about humans. Employees and colleagues represent the greatest assets for your enterprise security, and the greatest threats to it (along with human threat actors on the outside).

Here, we're going to look at a few principles that I have found invaluable when hiring and retaining talent for threat intelligence positions. I call them the three P's: patience, perseverance, and positivity, and the three C's: curiosity, creativity, and communication. Those are joined by what I think are the essential qualities of management, the three E's: emotional intelligence, empathy, and execution.

Hiring Talented Professionals

In 2020, hiring and retaining talented security employees is a challenge. Because demand far outpaces supply, millions of jobs remain unfilled.[31] The following rules apply for hiring in any industry, but they are doubly important for the cybersecurity industry, where turnover in skilled roles can be particularly damaging to the bottom line.

When you interview cybersecurity candidates, try to establish a realistic picture of their work ethic and their technical skills. One of my favorite questions for security operations (blue

---

31 Shirley Tay, CNBC, *A serious shortage of cybersecurity experts could cost companies hundreds of millions of dollars*: https://www.cnbc.com/2019/03/06/cybersecurity-expert-shortage-may-cost-companies-hundreds-of-millions.html

team) positions is, "Tell me what happens when you type google.com into your laptop's web browser and hit 'enter.'" It's an open-ended question, and the level of answer depth is indicative of the candidate's understanding of operating system processes and internet protocols.

Over the years, I've received a couple of great answers where the candidates launched into a detailed exposition of the domain name system (DNS), internet routing via border gateway protocol (BGP), and the detailed mechanics — at different layers of the OSI model — that support a successful connection between a laptop and a Google-owned server.

I've also received answers that began with a pause, a long "um," followed by a very brief summary of how web browsers and web servers connect to each other. Obviously, candidates experience nervousness and knowledge recall isn't always perfect, but when scoring general technical skills there's a correlation between the comprehensiveness of answers to this type of open-ended question and the candidate's experience.

Goodness in Threes

There are a few core virtues that I believe are even more valuable in a candidate than mere technical knowledge and skill. Technical skills can be learned in junior roles, and this industry is evolving so quickly that employees who don't adopt an attitude of humility and demonstrate an eagerness to keep learning will be left behind. What can't be taught so easily are core values like the three P's and the three C's.

The Three P's

The proliferation of social media, on-demand entertainment, and interrupt-driven workflows are contributing to shorter attention spans and general restlessness. Patience and perseverance are two critical qualities in a field that can be frustrating and challenging and leave participants in a state of constant exasperation. Technological progression never stops, which means security is a career-long learning engagement. In my experience, patience and perseverance are the fundamental ingredients for success, regardless of the challenge.

The three P's: patience, perseverance, and positivity

Positivity is more than a "nice to have" in a security team. Positivity doesn't mean ignoring negative events and circumstances; rather, it's a commitment to consistently putting forth the best effort, producing the best work, and creating the best team. It's a commitment to acknowledge and address negative sentiments, including negative comments and feedback, while focusing on causation and solutions. It's rarely straightforward to identify candidates with a positive disposition solely through interviews, but it helps to ask for examples of times they have overcome unusual challenges. You should also follow up with references and ask them for situations where the candidate did, or did not, exhibit the three P's.

The prior three characteristics are positive, but it's worth mentioning the inverse negative qualities that can destroy team morale. Former Treasury Secretary Timothy Geithner once warned against them through his policy: "no jerks, no whiners, no peacocks."

I know from firsthand experience that oversized egos can severely disrupt a team's productivity and morale. A lack of humility leads to jerk-like behavior. Whining is a habit that can be caught and corrected, but a "peacock" is difficult to reform because too much ego impedes an individual's ability to receive feedback. Worse, a human peacock feels entitled and superior to colleagues. Nothing will corrode team unity quicker than an unrepentant peacock.

The Three C's

Where the three P's are important for all jobs, the three C's — creativity, curiosity, and communication — are especially important in information security. Creativity in problem solving is a desirable attribute in any candidate. Curiosity is equally important. If candidates aren't self-motivated to understand technical concepts and mechanisms, then their ability to solve problems creatively is diminished.

The three C's: curiosity, creativity, and communication

The importance of the third C — communication — can't be overstated. Historically, HR consultants and employment pundits have referred to verbal and written communication as "soft skills." This is a misnomer. Even the most extroverted people must work to master writing and presenting skills. Hard communication skills are non-negotiable for success and career growth.

Also, productivity within teams depends on basic communication skills. Security professionals must be able to communicate facts and dates for project delivery, set and manage expectations during projects, and interact smoothly with peers, managers, and direct reports.

A good request for candidates is to "provide an example of a time when your communication failed, what you learned, and how you changed." This is not a gotcha question like "What are your weaknesses?" Everyone fails at communication sometimes, and understanding what the candidate learned will provide insight into his or her level of self-awareness and recognition of the importance of communication skills.

Retaining Talented Professionals

Hiring well and onboarding new hires effectively are resource-intensive activities. It's in an organization's best interest to retain professionals who are so costly to attract and employ.

This is doubly true for security professionals because there's always another job over the horizon with better compensation. No organization can afford to lose its top security performers. Not only is that costly, it's dangerous. When institutional knowledge of IT/OT systems and security controls departs, the organization becomes more vulnerable to attacks and operational risks increase.

Although the employer/employee relationship is transactional rather than familial, today's employers must go out of their collective way to create cultures that build communities with shared purpose and values that include trust, respect, and inclusivity.

It is incumbent upon those who directly manage people to view them as humans, not headcount. This distinction is important when planning for hiring, forced relocations, and layoffs.

The Three E's of Leadership

Managers manage people, projects, and processes. Leaders build mutual respect and trust that lead to improved execution.

Leaders are selfless in helping their team solve challenges, and they serve the broad needs of the collective unit. They confidently set the tone for the pace and pursuit of organizational goals. They reinforce the team's purpose. In short, they articulate the "why."

The three E's — emotional intelligence, empathy, and execution — are leadership requirements to build trust and successful organizations.

Emotional intelligence is the ability to understand people and their motivations. Understanding begins with active listening. Everyone has something to say, and leaders are often exceptionally good at listening, processing ideas, and thinking before speaking. Non-verbal information is just as crucial to collect and understand. Body language and vocal tone can offer important clues about an individual's mental state and job satisfaction.

The three E's: emotional intelligence, empathy, and execution

Empathy is related to but distinct from emotional intelligence. Empathy is the ability to mentally insert yourself into another's situation and feel what that individual is feeling. Employees are people with personal lives first and work lives second. The range of experiences and issues that people live with are immense, including marriages, births, deaths, illness, incarceration, financial hardship, and separation. To empathize is to recognize the enormous effects created by personal events and respond with appropriate emotions like compassion, joy, and sorrow.

Execution is the third critical component. Successful businesses tend to be data driven. Anecdotes may be helpful, but there is strength in empirical data. Great leaders obtain necessary data to make decisions, gauge team members, and monitor program effectiveness. Intense execution of a strong strategy propels teams and the wider organization to be successful. Leadership begins with a commitment to execute the organization's vision and mission.

Maintaining a Strong Culture

When determining whether to stay in a role or to accept a new one, cybersecurity professionals consider many variables in addition to compensation. Surveys show that company and team culture play a huge role in employee retention.

- Building blocks essential to creating a culture of mutual respect and trust include:
- Support for co-workers
- Regular feedback
- Recognition of jobs done well
- Training and professional growth opportunities
- Mental health breaks

Training and professional growth opportunities are critical because technology and security are evolving at breakneck speeds. Cybersecurity professionals will feel that they are falling behind the knowledge curve unless they are provided with ample opportunities to learn, train, and network with industry peers.

Management attitudes and HR systems need to provide "mental health breaks" so employees can avoid burnout and the pressures of 24/7 communication by taking personal time away from work to unplug (ideally with no email or texts).

Automation is a valuable goal, but humans will always be required for specific security workflows. Creating an environment where professionals can thrive will benefit organizations and reduce risk in the long term.

Chapter 10

The Security Intelligence Lifecycle and Workflow

on't you love simplicity? When was the last time you heard someone ask for more complexity? We all want more simplicity in business and in life.

Cybersecurity is one field where complexity can quickly overwhelm the practitioners. Explaining technical concepts like public key encryption is straightforward, but concepts relating to business value are much harder to describe, as we've seen throughout this book.

To simplify security practices we need a few simple frameworks and workflows to define our processes, help us set goals, and measure the results of our actions. I want to discuss two frameworks here that will help summarize some of the thoughts and recommendations I've presented throughout the book.

The first is a straightforward framework of three (and a half) steps that can guide decisions from a business value standpoint, which uses business value to guide cybersecurity decisions. The second is a security intelligence lifecycle, which codifies much of the guidance I've given about goal-setting and explores how people in the roles I discussed in the last chapter can work together to create intelligence that leads to operational outcomes that reduce risk.

A Workflow for Risk Management

There is a three-step framework that can align cybersecurity processes and goals with business value. This framework isn't new — its steps are axiomatic in business today— but it's not always used in the cybersecurity domain. The three steps are:

1. Identify a threat
2. Take action
3. Measure and communicate the value of the action

But this framework has not been very effective in cybersecurity. Why is that?

As we have been discussing, it's at least partly because cybersecurity professionals and enterprise managers are not speaking the same language. Security people are primarily concerned with business enablement and act to ensure businesses can operate without interruption. C-suite executives and members of the board of directors are more concerned with profitability. Those at the top of the organization often see cybersecurity investments only as cost centers that drag down the bottom line. That's why step three, "measure and communicate the value of the action," is the most challenging — and also the most necessary.

To bridge the gap, security professionals must measure and communicate the value of security controls in the language of risk. They can accomplish this by introducing a half-step between steps one and two of the framework. The revised workflow, looks like this:

1. Identify a threat
   a. Determine if the threat is a risk
2. Take action
3. Measure and communicate the value of the action

Unfortunately, as I talk with security professionals and enterprise executives across many industries, I find that this approach is opposed or ignored in favor of threat- or compliance-driven security practices. Many people resist change, and often leaders are unwilling to invest in measuring risk levels before and after actions against threats are taken. We need a way to get everybody on the same page and communicate using the same terms. To apply this risk workflow more specifically to the production of security intelligence, we'll turn to the next framework I want to talk about: the security intelligence lifecycle.

The Security Intelligence Lifecycle

Intelligence is built on analytic techniques honed over several decades by government and military agencies. Traditional intelligence focuses on six distinct phases that make up what is called the "intelligence cycle": direction, collection, processing, analysis, dissemination, and feedback.

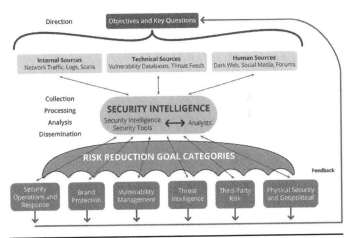

Security intelligence and the six phases of the intelligence lifecycle. (Source: Recorded Future)

Before we get into the steps of the lifecycle, I want to point out how the risk workflow I discuss above complements it (or should). You might notice that in many ways the two run parallel to each other. However, if the lifecycle of intelligence helps us to better understand how intelligence is produced, the risk workflow helps answer why.

> *If the lifecycle of intelligence helps us to understand how intelligence is produced, the risk workflow helps answer why.*

The security intelligence lifecycle seems straightforward, and certainly many organizations follow it closely and produce well-researched intelligence on a regular schedule. Someone in a leadership role, or perhaps a client, sets out a research goal for the team, and the analysts gather data from various sources, analyze it, and write reports, which they present to the people who asked for that research. To perform these tasks, organizations often create a well-oiled (and expensive) machine, made up of many highly trained and well-educated analysts using various advanced, costly security solutions. The "how" gets done with hard work and expertise. Then what happens? What are the operational outcomes? Who really reads those reports and does anything meaningful with them?

The Threat Category Risk framework provides guidance that enables enterprises to stop wasting time and money producing intelligence that doesn't lead to meaningful operational outcomes. It provides the "why" so that:

- In the direction phase of the lifecycle, goals can be set based on risks, not just identified threats

- The collection, processing, and analysis of information can be oriented toward intelligence that will reduce risk in ways that can be measured based on financial cost

- The intelligence reports that are produced from that analysis present findings in the language of risk and costs so they are readily understood by decision-makers

- Results can be fed into the next cycle of decision-making, goal-setting, and intelligence production, rather than sitting unread on desks or unopened in inboxes

Breaking Down the Security Intelligence Lifecycle

Direction

In the direction phase, leaders set goals and parameters for a cycle of intelligence-gathering. The goals may be in response to a request from a client within the organization, a news story, an internal alert, or a proactive decision to improve some aspect of cybersecurity.

Setting goals within a risk-centered framework involves understanding and articulating:

- The information assets and business processes that need to be protected
- The potential impacts of losing those assets or interrupting those processes
- The types of intelligence that the security organization requires to protect assets and respond to threats
- Priorities about what to protect

Once high-level intelligence needs are determined, an organization can formulate questions that can be answered in specific, measurable terms. For example, we can look back at our example in Chapter 3 of estimating the risk posed to our enterprise by credential reuse. For one cycle of intelligence-gathering, we might want to set goals that would help us more accurately estimate the potential risk posed by credential reuse attacks to our organization.

Collection

The next step is to gather information to address those intelligence requirements. Information can be gathered in a variety of means and from various sources including:

- Pulling metadata and logs from internal networks and security devices
- Subscribing to threat data feeds from industry organizations and cybersecurity vendors
- Holding conversations and targeted interviews with knowledgeable sources
- Scanning open source news and blogs
- Scraping and harvesting websites and forums
- Infiltrating closed sources such as dark web forums

Today, the collection stage is best done by machines, leaving humans free to focus on analysis. For our example of credential reuse, it would be helpful to determine whether any employee credentials have been leaked through credential dumps, and if so, to determine whether those leaked credentials are appearing for sale in criminal marketplaces. Monitoring those sources and collecting information from them manually is nearly impossible to do at scale, but automated solutions have no problem doing so.

The collection stage is best done by machines, leaving humans free to focus on analysis.

Processing

Processing is the stage where all of that unsorted information is categorized and transformed into a format that readily lends itself to analysis. This step, too, can often be handled by an automated solution.

For example, processing might involve extracting indicators of compromise from an email, enriching them with other information, and then communicating with endpoint protection tools for automated blocking. A human analyst would have to painstakingly look up each indicator, but the same enrichment process can be performed easily by a security intelligence solution that has near-instant access to the breadth of information on the internet.

Analysis

Analysis is where humans shine and machines generally don't. This is the stage where information is evaluated within the context of the goals set out in the first stage of the lifecycle and recommendations to reduce risk are made. Analysis might produce recommendations to investigate a potential threat, to act immediately to block an attack, to strengthen security controls, or to invest in additional security resources.

Whatever the goal, the form in which the information is presented is especially important. It must be in a format that the reader understands, as I've emphasized throughout the book. For analysts who are communicating with business executives, this is best done through the language of risk. For example, if you want to communicate with non-technical leaders, your report must:

- Be concise (a one-page memo or a handful of slides)
- Avoid confusing and overly technical terms and jargon

- Articulate the issues in business terms (such as direct and indirect costs and impact on reputation)
- Include a recommended course of action

Dissemination

Dissemination involves getting the finished intelligence output to the places it needs to go. Most cybersecurity organizations have multiple teams that can benefit from security intelligence, which are enumerated in the diagram above.

For each of these audiences, you need to ask:

- What intelligence do they need, and how can external information support their activities?
- How should the intelligence be presented to make it easily understandable and actionable for that audience?
- How often should we provide updates and other information?
- Through what media should the intelligence be disseminated?
- How should we follow up if they have questions?

Some intelligence may need to be delivered in a variety of formats for different audiences, say, by a live video feed or a PowerPoint presentation. Not all intelligence needs to be presented in a formal report. Successful threat intelligence teams provide continual technical reporting to other security teams with external context around IOCs, malware, threat actors, vulnerabilities, and threat trends.

Feedback

It's critically important to understand your overall intelligence priorities and the requirements of the security teams that will be consuming the intelligence. Their needs guide all phases of the intelligence lifecycle and tell you:

- What types of information to collect
- How to process and enrich that information

- How to analyze the information and present it as actionable intelligence
- To whom each type of intelligence must be disseminated, how quickly it needs to be disseminated, and how fast to respond to questions

You need regular feedback to make sure you understand the requirements of each group, and to make adjustments as their requirements and priorities change.

Successful Business Is Risk Management

We have reached the end of the book, so I will say it one more time: Always develop cybersecurity requirements and priorities through a risk-centric framework.

Set goals using the three and a half steps of the workflow outlined here. Make those goals specific, manageable, and measurable so that you can easily see the results. Don't be afraid to make adjustments as needed. You won't always make the right call the first time, and that's okay, because in an industry where threat actors' tactics, techniques, and procedures are always shifting and evolving, getting stuck in the same routines and maintaining the status quo can be fatal.

> *Don't be afraid to make adjustments as needed. You won't always make the right call the first time, and that's okay.*

You'll never completely eliminate risk, but if you follow these steps you will absolutely reduce it and produce benefits you can measure.